THE
NEW
JAPANESE
HOUSE

Chris Fawcett

THE NEW JAPANESE HOUSE

Ritual and Anti-Ritual

Patterns of Dwelling

ICON EDITIONS

HARPER & ROW, PUBLISHERS, New York

Cambridge, Hagerstown, Philadelphia, San Francisco,
London, Mexico City, São Paulo, Sydney

1817

FIRST U.S. EDITION

ISBN: 0-06-433010-9

LIBRARY OF CONGRESS CATALOG CARD NUMBER: 80-8224

81 82 83 84 10 9 8 7 6 5 4 3 2 1

CONTENTS

ACKNOWLEDGEMENTS

Such a book as this is indebted to many people whose ideas, encouragement, translation, criticism, editing and draughting have made this a reality. The Japanese Ministry of Education, whose scholarship enabled this study to be begun, Kazumasa Yamashita, whose office tolerated my presence for six months, the guiding hands of Makoto Uyeda, Nobuko Morita, the translation skills of Akiyoshi Hirayama, Kumiko Shimada, the enthusiasm of Prof. Tomoya Masuda of Kyoto University and assistants Kunio Kato and Tamikoshi, the clowning seriousness of Monta Mozuna and Toyokazu Watanabe, the rigour of Hiromi Fujii's conversations, the enthusiasm of Dalibor Veseley and Peter Carl, the editorial skills of Dennis Sharp; but most of all, thanks must go to Gunther Nitschke, at whose East Asian Institute for the Anthropology of Building Anthropology, I first got an inkling as to what it was all about. ADA Edita, under the brilliant photographer Yukio Futagawa, published the essay, in GA Houses 4: expanded and put into more of a context, it has formed the nucleus of this book, and I am indebted to his impetus.

Illustration Sources

The author wishes to thank the following for providing the illustrations listed:

Takefumi Aida: pages 111, 141, 142; Tadao Ando: pages 130, 131, 132, 133, 134, 135, 136; Masao Arai: page 147 (right); Takamitsu Azuma: pages 102, 103, 104, 105; Tony Barter: page 54; Mitchel Bring: page 30; John Clark: page 10; Dam Dan: page 114 (bottom); Redrawn from GA Houses, No 4, 1978, ADA Edita Tokyo: pages 19, 23, 107, 108; Hiroshi Hara: pages 85 (right), 86, 87, 88, 89, 92, 93, 95; Itsuko Hasegawa: pages 150 and 151; Akiyoshi Hirayama: pages 99 (bottom), and 115 (right); Tomotsune Honda:

pages 44 and 113 (right); Tomotsune Honda and Yasuyori Yada: page 57 (bottom); Arata Isozaki: page 170; Toyō Ito: page 139; Redrawn from *Japan Architect* (J.A.), July 1971: page 61; and J.A. 7604: page 169; Itsuo Kamiya: page 119; Shin Komakine: page 56; Akira Komiyama: page 51 (bottom), 100 and 148; Isamu Kujirai: page 115 (left); Tatsuhiko Kuramoto: page 128 (left); Hiroshi Misawa: page 114 (top); Monta Mozuna: pages 157, 158, 159, 160, 162 and 163; Osamu Murai: page 147 (left); Kiyoshi Nakagome: page 166; Kijo Rokkaku: pages 116, 117, 118, 120; Kiyoshi Sakurai: page 53; G. B. Sansom, translator, The Tsuredure Gusa, Transactions of the Asiatic Society of Japan, vol xxxix, 1911: page 75; Kumiko Shimada: pages 48 and 85 (left); Redrawn from *Space Design* (S.D.) Special Issue 6, 1974: page 90; Yutaka Suzuki: page 99 (top); Shin Takamatsu: pages 60, 124, and 125; Minoru Takeyama: pages 21 and 126; Redrawn from *Toshi Jutaku* (T.J.) 7408: page 45; Redrawn from T.J. 7010: page 42; Yuzuru Tominaga: pages 96, 97, 98 and 146; Toyokazu Watanabe: pages 16, 22, 36, 57 (top), 144, 145, 172 and 173; Yōji Watanabe: pages 15, 35, 112, and 113 (left); C. A. S. Williams, *Outlines of Chinese Symbolism and Art Motives*, Kelly and Walsh, 1932: page 82; Redrawn from Y. Yamamoto, Namahage, Institute for the Study of Human Issues, Philadelphia, 1978: page 51 (top); Eiji Yamane: page 101; Redrawn from Kunio Yanagita, *Nenchu Gyōji Zusetsu* (A Pictorial Guide to Ceremonies Throughout the Year), Iwasaki Shoten, Tokyo, 1964 and Yaeko Shiotsuki, Zukai Kankon Sosai, (Illustrating the Four Main Ceremonies), Kobunsha, Tokyo, 1976: pages 67 and 72; Redrawn from Yanagita, *op cit*, and Yanagita, Yukiguni no Minzoku (Snow Country Folklore), Yotkusha, Tokyo, 1944: page 74; Yasuo Yoshida: page 109 (left), 153, 154, 155, 167; The illustrations on pages 13, 14, 34, 38, 39, 43, 46, 50, 52, 64, 66, 68, 70, 73, 76, 77, 78, 79, 80, 109 (three photographs on right), 110, 126, 128 (right) and 168, were all provided by the author.

DO WE LIVE TO BUILD OR BUILD TO LIVE? . . . towards an ontology of the new Japanese house.

A sizzling trip by Shinkansen, the bullet-train, to Tokyo to clarify some details with the editor who had invited me to write this in its first version. An afternoon's discussion with him about the architects he wanted me to include. That night, after drinking sacred *sake* which the architect Monta Mozuna had brought back from the building ceremony celebrating the raising of the ridge pole of an office building of his own design, five or six of us slept in his office. I had a dream – all the architects I was due to write about appeared floating in mid-air, flying in mandala formation at bullet-train speed.

PRELIMINARIES

During World War II 'Full-scale models of Japanese houses were designed and built in New Jersey and assembled at the Utah Proving Grounds for experimental bombing purposes.' (1)

After his 1963 trip East, Peter Smithson, in his Michael Ventris talk at the Architectural Association, London, entitled 'Form Above All', characterised Japanese object-making and place-making as the embodiment of a 'rectangular plane and a certain sort of curve'; 'mastering volumes', 'uncrossable rectangles', 'interior spaces both inside and out' (2) – such phrases proliferated in his address.

These comments typify the stock images of Japan and its buildings that the Western architect has long nourished: 'Temple', 'House', 'Garden', 'Castle', 'Ise', 'Katsura', and more recently 'Metabolism' and its sibling 'Post-Metabolism'. But these stereotypes are in fact a bunch of isolates wilfully grabbed from the authentic Japanese environment, which is a lived continuum from metropolis to *tatami* mat, from cosmos to column. What has made it possible for us to mistake this hotch-potch of figments of our Western imagination for the real thing is the deep rooted misconceptions by which we surround the 'exotic'. There has been an historical tendency for the true nature of the 'exotic', the 'oriental', the 'eastern', to be defused and for its meaning to be rarefied behind armourplate glass walls in museums or in the glossy prints of picture-books. Deprived of its original ground, the exotic item is only permitted a single function, that of titillation – it cannot enter our lives in the same way it entered into the life of its host environment. The Japanese house, or a Post-Metabolist project appears monstrous to us, if not outright miraculous, for these specimens are presented to us in arty volumes which eschew any reference to the home culture which succoured them and without which

A farmhouse near Murōji, Nara Prefecture

Shūgakuin Detached Palace, Kyoto . . . (*Sukiya-zukkuri* style)

Katsura Detached Palace, South Kyoto . . . (*Shoin-zukkuri* style)
The West's 'Japanese House' is a curious amalgam of bits indiscrimately derived second- and third-hand from these house types

they could no longer be. That a Japanese house does not appear grotesque and outlandish to the people who live in it should be enough of a warning – the house does not exist as something unto itself but engages in a daily exchange of social, economic and ritual gestures, and any attempt by the Western architect to try to come to terms with the Japanese house must start from this basic anthropological understanding.

By examining the new Japanese house we shall have a good chance of airing some of these issues, and perhaps *perspectise* some of our more longstanding presuppositions. By way of introduction, we might briefly ponder on how these stock images have been propagated.

The Japanese infatuation

'a drop of their blood has mixed with our blood and no power on earth can eliminate it.' (Louis Gonse, *Le Japon Artistique*, 1888)

The arrival of Commodore Perry in Japan in 1853 was an attempt to bring to an end the epochs of idle Western speculation concerning that remote and inhospitable place: seamen's tales and fantastic guesswork had built up in the Westerner's eye a fabulous picture of mythical beasts and surreal landscapes. Missionary reports had achieved little better, portraying the country as a primitive refuge of all manner of superstition and idolatory. The opening up of Japan had many consequences.

Japanese prints were first brought to Europe by the Dutch traders from Nagasaki in about 1815 but it was the 1853 treaty with America and the British treaty negotiated by Elgin in 1858 which brought serious attention to these works. Captain Sherard Osborn, in 1861, published a book on Japan in which he refers to Hiroshige as 'our embryo Turner' and comments on the 'Hogarth-like talent of Japanese artists'. Such prints were shown at the International Exhibition of 1862 in London and at the Paris exhibition of 1867; while in the same year, the Goncourts began their collection of prints. What had begun as a fashion soon became a craze. By the end of the nineteenth century many European artists had felt the influence of the Japanese print, among them Whistler, Beardsley, Toulouse-Lautrec, and Degas. Van Gogh, who owned prints by some of the later artists, actually transcribed into oil paintings certain plates from Hiroshige's 'Hundred Views of Edo'. In Paris in the 1880s, *Le Divan Japonais* had become the most popular haunt of the art world.

After centuries of isolation, or 'proud loneliness', with Perry's arrival, Japan found itself faced outwards, no longer inwards. The Meiji Reformation of 1868 gave added impetus to this process of externalisation. The *fin de siècle* saw the diffusion of Japanese objects throughout the West, featuring strange caprices in their ornamentation, violating the old proprieties; as for the utility of these objects, there was great confusion . . .

> We found it difficult to formulate the principles upon which such art was based, and yet were compelled to recognize its merit. But it did offer a way out of such objects, for example, as a child in brass, kneeling in supplication on a brass cushion, adroitly balancing on its head a receptacle for kerosene oil; we were no longer doomed to wipe our feet on cupids, horns of plenty, restless tigers or scrolls of architectural magnitude. (Morse)

It was an answer to the oppression of the orders, pattern books and classical design canons, much as Chinoiserie had been a century earlier, when at the height of that particular picnic, pagodas were arising throughout Europe, tentatively interpreted, but then, the West's romance with the orient has always been through a rose-coloured radio-telescope.

The modern architect's yearning for Japan: the new obligation

(. . . the irony has been that while we in the West were striving for the extensivity of Japanese space, the Japanese architect was striving for the more ruthlessly edited space of the West . . .)

It is the way certain images of Japan have insinuated themselves into our environmental being that has come to mean 'Japan' for us today. Japan is not a concrete reality that imposes on us in our day to day dealings, but is a factor that creeps in, colouring here and there our interpretations of 'environment'. Rykwert has pointed out the various constructs of a very arbitrary and intuitively obtained image of 'primitive hut' and the bearing it has had on the course of architectural history. Just so with the 'Japanese house' – its importance rests not on what it is in itself, but is a result of the scenario it has written for the Western architect over the last century. So, whatever it is we as architects in the West are working on, it is bound to refer as much to 'Japanese house' as to 'primitive hut'. (Just the whispering of the word 'Katsura' is enough to send shivers up and down the architect's spine.) 'Primitive hut', 'Japanese house' – one could think of other paradigms similarly enshrined in the working architect's degrees of consciousness – 'house-on-a-hill', 'house-by-the-sea', 'the-double-house', 'house-of-the-dead' . . . the architect's meta-cognisance of these exemplars are what guide his design hand to this day. It became customary for the modern architect to make an appeal to the Japanese house as the ultimate authority, the ultimate judgement – Katsura thus stands before us all, every column, eave, window spelling out jurisdiction over our inmost being.

What was it then about the Japanese house that aroused so many passions? Perhaps first and foremost, the modern architect looked to the Japanese house as being located in a heroic zone equidistant from function and form. Then, the absence of ornament married well with the Loosian position, while the subordination of form to the essentials of material cohered with the new creeds searching for alternative rationalities; the oneness of furnishings and structure appealed to Wright no less than its screened space. The traditional 'parts' method of construction, by which a house could be erected or dismantled bone by bone was also very tempting. It was realised that a bringing together of modular units, standardised components and finishes need not equal 'machine' . . . but the lesson was forgotten, and now the architect looks sorrowfully upon the Japanese house with a longing intensified by the publication of an ever increasing number of Japanese picture-books.

But in fact, does the 'Japanese house' as we know it actually exist? Going to Japan, the Western architect can spend his whole time there hunting feverishly for it in vain – what he is searching for is an engram, something firmly fixed in the secondary and tertiary

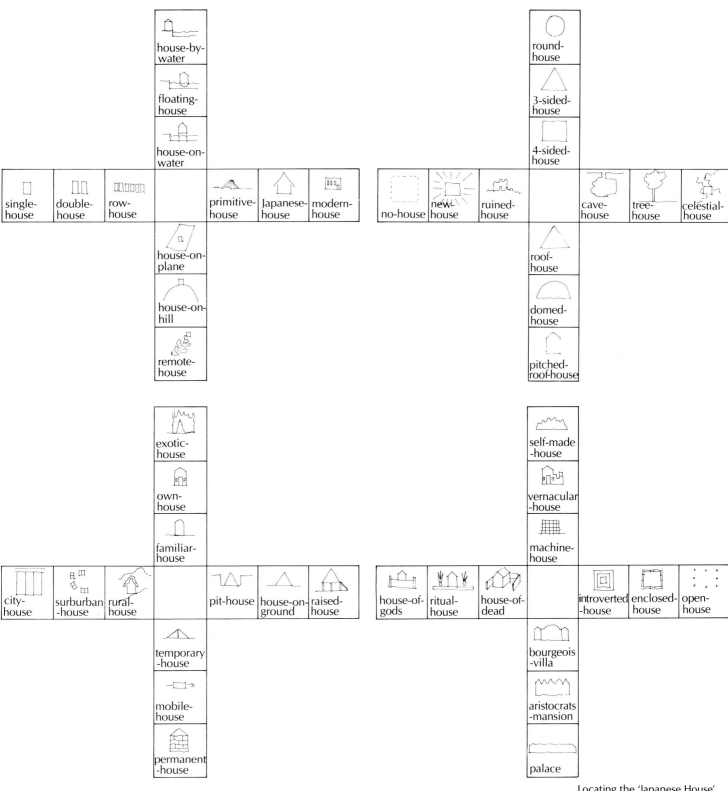

Locating the 'Japanese House' among the other house archetypes

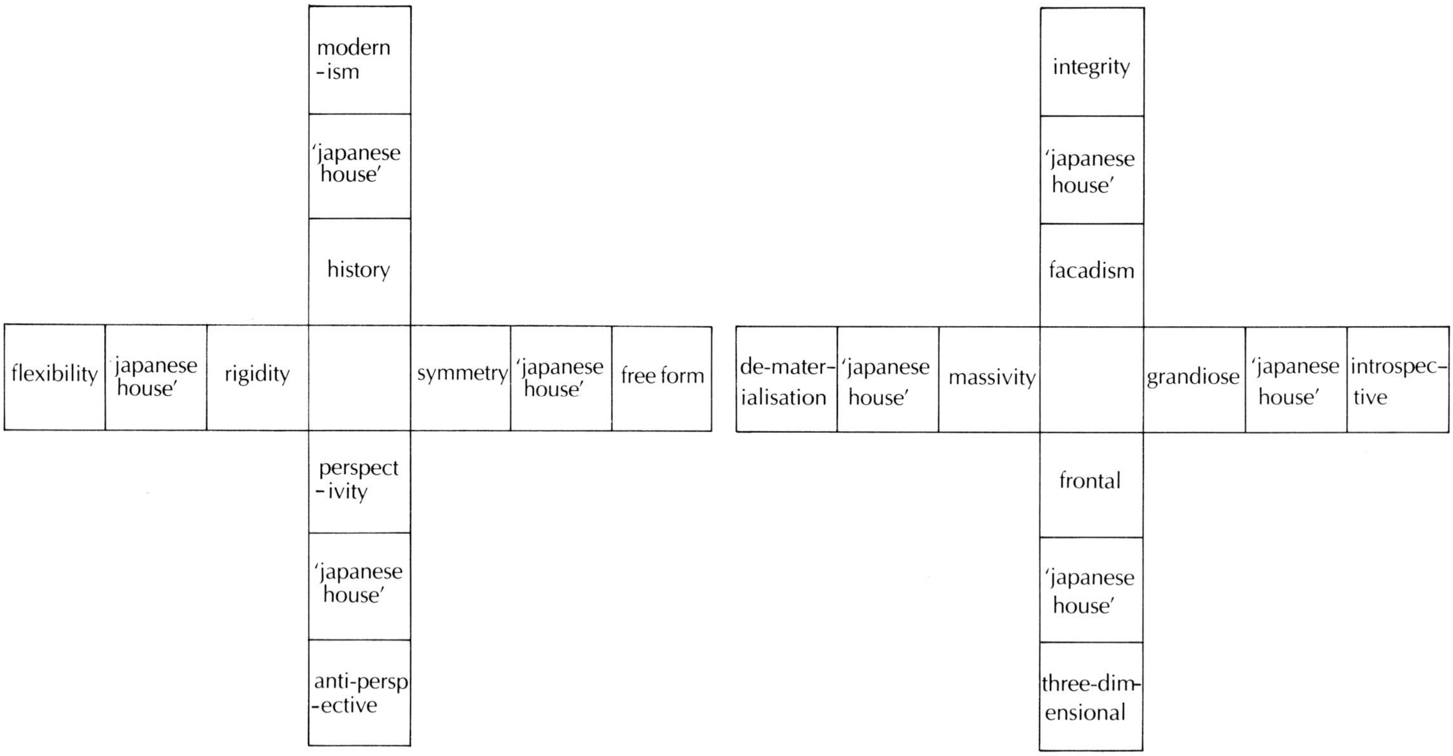

Left diagram:

```
                    modern-ism
                    'japanese house'
                    history
flexibility | japanese house | rigidity |        | symmetry | 'japanese house' | free form
                    perspect-ivity
                    'japanese house'
                    anti-persp-ective
```

Right diagram:

```
                    integrity
                    'japanese house'
                    facadism
de-materialisation | 'japanese house' | massivity |        | grandiose | 'japanese house' | introspective
                    frontal
                    'japanese house'
                    three-dimensional
```

The metamorphosis of historicism into modernism, and the pivot role played by the 'Japanese House'. Now, of course, the swing is the other way – façadism, massivity, history, perspective are re-ascendant; for the while, the Japanese paradigm rests off stage, rehearsing a new act it can present when fate once more beckons it on

environments (of the media and one's imagination), not the primary environment . . . he could find it more easily in any library. It is a coffee-table reverie, the outcome of our own rootedness, our own insularity, our own cultural inertia, and is exploited by the JAL advert and embassy literature. Perhaps we might conclude that the Japanese house does not exist, but is rather a product of our collective fantasising – I went looking for it, terrified it might even be there.

In the traditional Japanese house, adaptability, structural cogency, the modular disposition of dwelling events, simplicity, and the flow of an organic space with a domestic pulse, all found transliteration into modern architecture, and all have proven as unworkable in the raw as they have in Japan. The process, highlighted by the work of Boudon, whereby Corbusier's Pessac Housing was made more amenable to its occupants' notions of the good life is a process ongoing in every Japanese house; a daily engagement of local variation and adaptation. The longer one lives in Japan, the more one gets accustomed to the fact that a family does not live in strict accordance with the architectural 'facts' of their house, but across them, in a diagonal as it were. In contrast to our classicised, rarefied notions of what Japanese space should be, it is in fact a tricky and *ad hoc* domestic arena. In other words, the Japanese house does not exist – it is rather a flux, a cycle, a dynamic that in fact cannot be photographed – it has to be posed. The pulse slowed, a photo can arise, leading to the tranquillity we in the West have thought so long belonged to the space itself.

The modern architect saw in the Japanese house the 'division and distribution of pure surfaces', governed by principles of modular composition and a high degree of

Yōji Watanabe, Nishida House, Tokyo, 1966. Exterior
This is Watanabe's interpretation of Bruce Goff's interpretation of 'Japanese House'. It is analogous to the way the British spread their architectural word through the Empire, which was then re-interpreted in loco and re-imported back into its home culture in the form of exotic balustrades, 'verandah's . . .

standardisation. What he understood as an ingenious and super-rational devotion to the objective in the environment, was in the end a response to a highly ritualised perception – for example, the parts of a Japanese house had to be sympathetically arranged owing to the various *kami* (spirits, deities), presiding over a site. Site configuration, location, accessibility – all were handled in ritual terms. Space in the house was determined by a host of ceremonial requirements; places for making offerings were needed, and display spaces used in seasonal or annual festivals . . . so much for the Japanese house as an assembly of self-evident constituents . . . so much for the 'cleanness' Taut admired . . . so much for the chaste distinction between envelope and frame that Mies admired . . . so much for the 'elimination of the insignificant' that Wright had a predilection for . . . The Japanese house is a complex bag of cultural idiosyncrasies inaccessible to the architect in the West, whose cursory glance cast in its direction can only bounce off. It is exactly this ritual side of the Japanese house that will be one of the major themes of this book.

Expanding universe or steady state?

Another function of this text is to put into a more meaningful frame those much bandied terms 'Metabolism' and 'Post-Metabolism'. The latter will be viewed primarily through its houses and their roots in traditional Japanese domestic and ritual space. Although for the sake of convenience we shall be using this terminology, our reservations must be stated right away: the term 'Post-Metabolism' is particularly

Toyokazu Watanabe, Doctor's House and Surgery, Ibaraki City, 1974
Exterior
Underneath a soaring Renaissance dome is an independent, timber, shrine-like structure with a *tatami* floor. This house comments more acidly on the East/West dichotomy than Yōji Watanabe's comparable Nishida House.

loaded, implying a phenomenon like Post-Modernism, stepping out of the pages of yesterday's architectural encyclopedias and marching into today's. But we must not allow ourselves to think of architecture in terms of 'advance' and 'progress', but as a cyclic, recurrent drama reinterpreting bedrock issues drawn up in archetypal time. Architecture is far from a relentless bodying forth of styles in associated epochs; it is, rather, a restirring and re-serving of a cosmic stew, beyond time and place, ladled out into different reservoirs of consciousness. Architecture is not a mechanical 'expanding universe' but a 'steady state' world system occasionally recharged and replenished . . . 'psychoanalysis offers a theoretical framework for exploring the possibility of a way out of the nightmare of "progress" and endless Faustian discontent, a way out of the human neurosis, a way out of history . . . the method . . . is to deepen the historical consciousness of the individual (fill up the memory gaps) till he awakens from his own history as from a nightmare.' (3)

Metabolism

Metabolism had rocketed to pre-eminence in the 'sixties and early 'seventies, in the wake of Kikutake, Kurokawa, Maki and Ohtaka's joint manifesto of 1960; Tange and Isozaki's defection from a former Zen–Corbusian line to the Metabolist cause in 1964 was the final seal of warranty, and from then on there was no stopping it. Its appeal rested on the many analogical levels involved in its derivation: there was the biological analogy meant to replace the mechanical orthodoxy of modernism – buildings and cities were compared to the cycles of change, renewal and destruction of organic tissue. At another level, Metabolism was likened to the Buddhist vision of the world-in-transformation, where objects are not static reference points to which our experience refers, but are momentary configurations. This is close to the third analogical level, where Metabolism can be seen as embodying the sensitivity to nature and its changing demands that is bound up with Shinto, the autochthonous, animistic Japanese religious root; the twenty year cycle of renewal of Ise Shrine, the primary Shinto sanctuary, is a hymn to this. And of course, we must not forget that most of the Metabolist programme – susceptibility of change between rooms, flexibility of function, and a reciprocity between inside and out – would always have been met by the building type the Metabolists were the most reticent about and conscience-striken over – the traditional Japanese house (in fact, Kenzo Tange was living in such a house, in the suburbs of Tokyo, until only very recently).

The commonplace verb of change in Japanese is *kawaru*; its Chinese character (*kanji*) is made up of a combination of two radicals – one is a simplification of the *kanji* representing 'entangled strings', while the other is a transformation of a sign of motion, representing the idea of holding a stick. Together, the *kanji* expresses the idea of rearranging or disentangling something which is confused or tangled, and generally means 'to change'. In other words, 'change' is regarded as an organisational principle, not something disruptive and fickle. It was this plateau of cultural agreement on which Metabolism was based, lending credibility to its vision of an environment as a sort of living plasma of demountable settings, a multi-strategy architecture of indeterminacy, in which the constituent parts 'moved like beasts of the sea, diminishing or increasing, going right or left, up or down, coalescing into colonies, dissolving into dust, solidifying into rocks, or softening to plankton.'

Metabolism's decline

But the situation in the 'sixties which allowed Metabolism to erect monuments to its cause, ironically contained the seeds of the Metabolist downfall. For that era of great consumer optimism, which saw for example the realisation of Tange's Yamanashi Press and Radio Centre, Kofu, 1967 and Kurokawa's Nakagin Capsule Tower, 1972, was accompanied by violent uprisings by students and farmers, who in their impatient and frantic search for some authentic values to live by, saw the Metabolist complexes as tokens of a feudal authority. The energy of this agitation went into halting the Metabolist's dream for the prismatic and formal concretisation of city, but it left a hiatus too. There was a pause, a lull; but slowly, it was recognised that simultaneous with and in opposition to the bittersweet turmoil of the Metabolist debate,other architects had been working along more private, introverted, small scale lines – Seichi Shirai (he had always followed an independent line of inquiry into what was expected of the architect in a greatly expanding urban tapestry – he made solemn and germanic buildings that established an almost occult influence over their surroundings, inducing calm into an otherwise inflated world) and Kazuo Shinohara (see below) were cases in point. There came a desire to elucidate what was essential to Japanese culture, as if this question had never been properly posed, let alone answered. A new resolve was set up by the Post Metabolists, to plumb Japan and its past to provide what might be a more exact model of what could be called distinctly Japanese. Concentrating on small singular houses, they found they could still enjoy the formal procedures embodied in the large scale Metabolist projects, but turned in more literary and ambiguous directions, affirming the architectural gesture as an idiosyncratic but necessary means of defining place. The architecture that grew was something to ponder; it was a means of thinking environment through, and marked a withdrawal from the world of Metabolism which had all the pretensions of an urban phenomenon but none of its bones – the extensive spaces in their projects which were left vacant, waiting for extensions and uncertain future demands, just gathered waste and began to decay.

Metabolism had, in its own way, tried to go against the divisiveness of the Japanese environment, but the projects failed one after the other, with no possibility of connection other than as successive pages in a magazine feature. On paper it looked convincing, but on the ground it died of embarrassment; the final demolition of the Expo '70 site, Osaka, in 1978, and the 1975 Ocean Expo, Okinawa, which turned into a wet dream when the intention had been a floating city, were the final two nails in the coffin. Post-Metabolism, accepting the tendency for walls to spring up without a moment's notice has found itself in a better position, which came to be consolidated.

Post-Metabolism also marked a necessary return to the enjoyment of architecture and its private small-scale passions, after the previous decade of rigorous, multi-scale civic complexes and fervent urbanist prayers. The emphasis has shifted from problem-

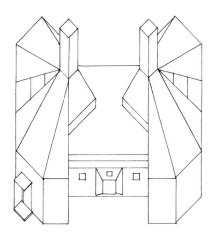

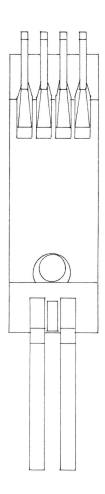

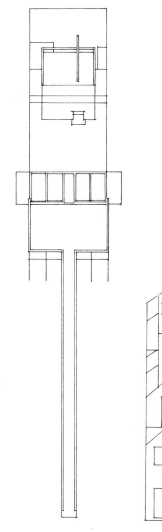

The last decade of attitudes towards 'house' has been lived autobiographically by every architect – here we see the change in mood of Toyō Itō. Upper left; left, a house in Tsujido, 1970; right, a house project of 1971. Upper right; left, a house in Sengataki; right, a house (Black Recurrence) in Sakarajosui, 1974. At the bottom; left, a house in Nakano, 1975–6; right, a house in Kamiwada, 1976. The end of the decade saw *gijutsu* (technique) and *shikata* (method) dominant, whereas of late *basho* (place) has come to the fore.

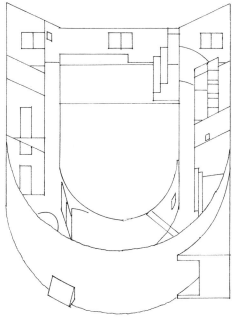

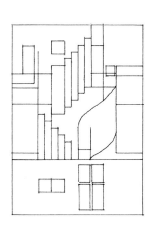

solving and network-analysis to more arcane areas of ritual and personal circumstance.

The eruption of Post-Metabolism

The exhibition 'Nine Japanese Architects' at the Architectural Association School, and the exhibition 'The New Wave In Japanese Architecture' that toured the U.S. recently, catalogued some of the latest developments since the discrediting of the 'Charred Ruins Metabolism' of Kurokawa, and Kikutake (who had experienced the destruction of Nagasaki and Hiroshima at an impressionable age) and since Tange's form of Metabolism had turned pretty rancid. The exhibitions were both a post-mortem with regard to the technological argument of a decade ago, and hinted at a few of the newer solutions being advanced, which include: the 'Shinohara School', represented for example by Itsuko Hasegawa and Issei Sakamoto, a self-styled 'blank-generation'; the architecture-of-the-absurd of Monta Mozuna and Tōyokazu Watanabe committing us to an eternity of cosmic conundrums; the ritual-affirming-architecture of Kazuhiro Ishii and Group Zō, playing up the ceremonial side. The point must be made – that the Post-Metabolist architecture of Japan is an astonished confirmation of the spasms, tensions and chasms of the metropolis. For Japan is a city, and its architecture is indistinguishable from the urban. What we can see there is an architecture-of-spectacle or alternatively 'architecture-versus-architecture', a 'Pleasure-House of the Rising Sun' perhaps, or more likely still a 'Cathedral of Erotic Misery'.

The main programme of Post-Metabolism

According to that special issue of *Japan Architect* which first coined the term 'Post-Metabolism', there are four main areas of interest on which Post-Metabolism has focused.

1. There is a rejection of the notion that architectural progress must go hand in hand with technical advance: Post-Metabolism posits a multivalued environment containing more different types of experience, organisation, etc., than technology alone can cope with. Hiroshi Hara, Monta Mozuna are good examples.

2. The second common point is that should the Post-Metabolist architect nonetheless want to take on an industrial theme, he employs the technical elements in an ironic manner – detaching these units from their ordinary technological implications, he fashions a very distinct context within which the building and its means of construction appear to point to quite different conclusions. Osamu Ishiyama, of the Dam-Dan group, is a good example.

3. Post-Metabolist architects reject the authenticity of large-scale, long-term civic proposals draughted by a single architect acting in vacuo – they insist, rather, on small-scale acts of urban subversion. Tadao Ando and Makoto Suzuki's blank living boxes, inserted into traditional urban areas, are provocative examples.

4. The fourth common point is that form depends on a cultural agreement, and cannot be insisted on from some pre-ordained vantage-point. Meaning cannot be

established beforehand with everything following on from that – it must come about in the man/building intercourse, it must be a living being – this is Atelier Zō's strength.

The basic distinctions could be listed thus:

Metabolism	*Post-Metabolism*
civic	cryptic
gargantuan	miniaturised
instrumental	existential
public accountability	private mythos
literal	allusive
expression of power	reverie quest
network	centre
tabulated self	performing self
indeterminate cartesian	genius loci

Minoru Takeyama, Hotel Beverly Tom, Hokkaido
The ritual-affirming stratum of Post-Metabolism is represented here . . . celebration, festivity, mardigras

Paradise will be the death of me (The Horizon of Immediate Phenomena)

The Voice Against Post-Metabolism
. . . 'we strut about in a bankrupt side-show playing parts we loathe to an audience whose values are meaningless or contemptible. Culture itself has become frippery and grease-paint. Our very revolutions are melodrama, performed under the stale rules of

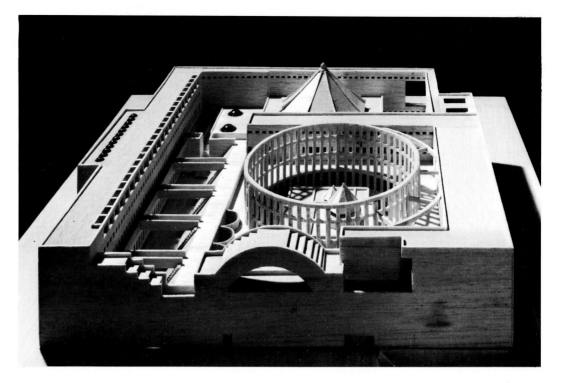

Toyokazu Watanabe, Dormitory
Project for a New Religion
View of the model
This project bears all the
hallmarks of the architecture-of-
the-absurd stratum of Post-
Metabolism. The dormitory rests
on a series of deliberately
unresolved oppositions;
Roman Coliseum: Japanese
bridge
Ottoman castle: Buddhist
octagonal temple roof

make-believe; they alter nothing but the cast . . .' (George Steiner).

Post-Metabolism can be objected to for manipulating material and space in contemptuous disregard of the strict facts at hand, for example, where concrete is treated flimsily, in conscious and ironic evocation of traditional devices; such precociousness could lead to a ready-made environment being thrust upon us as a *fait-accompli*, with no option on adaption. The consequent space arising from this provocative selection of window, wall and floor would be a distressing no-go-zone – 'manipulating space in a manipulating world' – these houses could be expecting too much of their occupants.

Another bone of contention is that the individual works of Post-Metabolism, like the bits of the Japanese city itself, do not come together, since there is no large scale structure guiding the overall geometry. There is the problem that the Post-Metabolist projects do not cohere in a larger metropolitan context – but this is a problem pertaining to Japan rather than Post-Metabolism itself. In Japan, each building becomes its own context, its own frame – the squares and crescents of London, for example, have no real equivalent – a building in Tokyo relates solely to the dynamics of its own genius loci. The recent group of typical commercial super-blocks in Shinjuku are a case in point – despite enjoying adjacent urban spots they do not even pretend to connect, rising as autonomous glacial slabs viewed in ghostly silhouette. Traditional taboos have restricted the joining of houses and even graves in rural Japan, although in the larger conurbations long rows of terrace housing had been built to rent to the labouring classes, but they disappeared in the late nineteenth century to be replaced by a more divisive type produced by a bourgeoisie thinking itself to be another Samurai class,

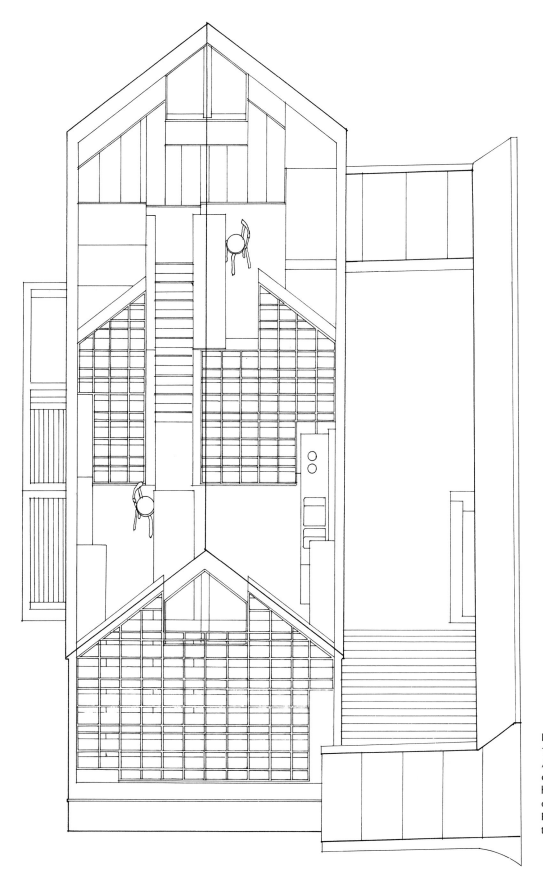

Kazunari Sakamoto, Project Y, 1976
A personal habitat in which the chairs, tables and other household effects prosper at the occupants' expense – typical of Post-Metabolism's other stratum, the Shinohara School

which had shared with the peasants a collective distaste for continuity and connection.

However much this 'bittiness', this 'environment in suspension' allows one to see architecture very vividly, one feels it is of less priority than sorting out the problems of city.

The critique aimed at Post-Metabolism is based on an uneasiness with regard to the manner in which the super-concentrates Tokyo, Osaka and Nagoya are, by some gyroscopic quirk, sucking up and absorbing, in increasing excitation, all alternative settlement patterns. What was felt to be peculiar to the Japanese system was that perhaps there was too little resistance offered to this homogenisation programme – and Post-Metabolism has little concern with these issues. The Japanese city, a restless image with a relentless appetite, encroaches on Japan unawares – the result? Japan-the-city. One must become worried that in the midst of this one-way process, the built-world would get fashioned into an all-embracing reality. The builders of this environment, technicians of the senses, engineers of the soul, take on issues of 'recognition', 'rivalry', 'conspicuousness', 'imitation', in a mad rush to see and be seen. One has no chance but to be the observer or the observed in this voyeuristic arcadia . . .

One is afraid that Post-Metabolism, though thinly disguised in a sentient form, is an architecture very much in the shape of death. In the rapid material deterioration of new buildings, in the rust stains, the ripped canvas awnings, the fading colours, Tokyo can easily become a city of ruin, inhabited by a populace beyond the penumbra. This is after all the logical conclusion to many traditional architectural values and their enthusiasm for decay. The resultant environment is divorced from the 'arc of existence', separated from the 'circle of immortality', far removed from the 'triangle of mortality', and ever farther removed from the 'spiral of history' or the 'parabola of eternity'; all we can see is the 'shape of death'.

Behind the scenes, something does not add up, and Post-Metabolism does not seem to be interested. In effect, hasn't Tokyo become the free-play of the commodity, its buildings being zeroed to 'Temples of Consumption'? Doesn't this kind of architecture operate by taking up the forces of production, lending them a medium whereby they can make themselves known as anything except that which they are? Aren't the contrasts and disjunctions just a 'put on', behind which capital continues its universally extensible ways? This book gives us a grandstand view, offering a timely opportunity to decide one way or the other.

Post-apocalyptic architecture (A Diminutive Body in Expanded Space)

The Case for Post-Metabolism
But of course, that is one view. The other is that the new Japanese environment by virtue of its ecstatic and delirious dreams of itself, by virtue of its sheer guts and determination, by virtue of its watchfulness and probity, is both positive affirmation and consummation of the Japanese metropolitan project. Its houses are particularly relevant.

We must defend Post-Metabolism as a timely emancipation from the tyranny of form – each project elevates an individual's ethic to the realm of pure, untrammelled architecture, at a level high above the crude juxtapositions of the industrial world.

Japanese society is running so fast it needs an architecture on the move, and in Post-Metabolism perhaps it has found it; this world-in-transit comprises a run-through of selections, with architecture as just one option, and style, logically, as an option of an option.

In the new Japanese explosion, the lexicon is Peter Cook's *Architecture Action and Plan*, but scrambled into a unique order. Architecture achieves a state of the most vivid free-fall of desires, a slalom run-through of every conceivable image; Tokyo assumes the role of a gas-station where history refuels itself. Architecture steps out of the cemeteries alive and well; prodigious panoramas unfolding, dioramas sent spinning, a palpitating vision of city and house.

CHAPTER ONE

ARCHITECTURE AND THE 'TECHNIQUES OF ECSTASY'

—A Personal Anthropology of the New Japanese Environment

Hito wa mikake ni yoranu mono.

. . . the young Japanese architect who went to Europe specially to get married in Ronchamp . . . this is no tall story . . .

Someone put it that modern architecture in the West began with housing, whereas in Japan it began with banks, city-halls, museums and the single house . . . Hence, for the Japanese architect, 'housing' is something completely beyond himself and is smothered over with all kinds of historical and political circumstances; the house, on the other hand is very much within reach . . . this is what makes the study of the new Japanese house so necessary. To get at the peculiarities of this house, one needs to follow two independent but mutually inclined ways – one with regard to the dynamics of the new environment as a whole and its precedents in the archaic Japanese environment; the other concerning the general nature of the house and the way its contemporary functions, particularly in Japan, correspond with many primordial functions . . . There are many grounds from which the Japanese house as it figures today has sprung, and it is my intention to examine some of the grounds as well as the figures.

(*scenario*): one day, when the architects of Tokyo and Osaka were quarrelling about architecture, Isozaki, holding up a cat, said 'You architects. If any of you can speak a word about architecture the cat will be spared, otherwise I will kill it.' No one could answer, so Isozaki killed it. Maeyakawa came back from somewhere and Isozaki told him what had happened. Maeyakawa took off his shoe, put it on his head and walked off. Isozaki said, 'If only you had been there, I could have saved the cat.'

Arrival

Since people coming to Japan from the West usually have such a strong preconception of what they are in for, during the customarily short period of their stay, that preconception is not modified in any way, but becomes also their ultimate perception. I was warned of this before coming, so tried to leave behind all such cultural baggage. This meant I arrived in a vulnerable condition . . . We docked at Yokohama early evening and it was darkening. We were met by Watanabe and drove off in the direction of Tokyo, dropping Gordon off at Shibuya before reaching Yamashita's design office, where I was to work for the next six months. Those things I describe fast so as to convey my total dependence on Watanabe, without whom the trip from Yokohama would have been an incandescent nightmare of trains, tubes, buses, connections . . . instead, relaxing somewhat in the front seat of the car, I was able to lose myself in the Tokyo images that mixed together on the windscreen and rear-view mirrors. The scene was a breathtaking one of disarticulation, as though the environment I had been familiar with in England had been put through a mincer; everything seemed out of control, one thing piled on top of another in dizzying perspectives, both vertical and horizontal, all around. A luridly illuminated panorama unrolled before me, like one of the Heian period scrolls I was to see later, depicting scenes from the Buddhist hell. There was no way of putting the pieces together to get any idea of the whole – it was a totally splintered universe of dissonances, a built equivalent of white noise. And yet it was intoxicating, promising dream beyond dream; my interior froze in wrought and delicate form at the prospect of what pleasures this place might have in store.

We drove on to Yamashita's office, but he was not there; while waiting for him, he phoned to invite us to a party celebrating the winners of a lighting design competition. We took a frenetic taxi to an immense hotel that seemed to salute as we went in; within seconds we made it, in a one *tatami* lift, to the 43rd floor and spilled out into the reception room, filled with celebrants, and at last I was able to meet this man who had helped me cross the world. A few minutes later we left, sharing the lift with Tange and Isozaki . . . already, Architecture was but a hair's breadth away. Next a cellar eating-place, *sake*, chopsticks, hitting my head on the low wooden beams, a rapid run through all these densely Japanese things. Back to Yamashita's for another bit of Architecture, this time the apartments he and some friends had got together to design and inhabit. Then on to Watanabe's house, where I was to stay in a *tatami* room, smelling of freshly cut grass, where I had to calculate each of my movements well in advance lest I injure any of the highly fragile surfaces . . .

The next day, my first full one in Japan, Watanabe went to his Institute, leaving me in the house alone. I sat comfortably but my heart was frozen. The chair was generous in its soft support, creating a nexus of gentle forces that held me in place, by my heart was frozen. The surface of the cushion was complementary to my skin, and its distribution was rather more around me than underneath, as though every square centimetre of me was thus supported, but my heart was frozen. I could move my head with ease, and let my eyes pass with unfixed gaze on the objects around – as I moved from left to right I could detect a sofa, a Sony speaker, an open door leading into the hall, a low square coffee table, three movable screens, two of which were drawn back to reveal a low dining-table with a small pit underneath to take the diners' legs and beyond a modern kitchen, then again to the right a drawing-board and chair, some heavy curtains and a large window which looked out onto a patio, a group of four chairs around a wood-slat table, a garden and beyond that apartment blocks stopping at the sky. I could have taken any one of these objects under scrutiny and subjected it to closer examination – the open door and its view into the hall, with its broad patterns of shadow on the green carpet and the generally receding tones, but that would have placed undue emphasis on that one object. What, instead, I must stress is the way they were all in cohesion, I must talk of the smoothness of the joints and junctions . . . I did not dare leave, for once out of here I might not be allowed back: I did not match the overall composition and would rupture the way one thing cohered with another . . . didn't I leave myself out of the inventory of objects?

When at last I managed to venture outside, crossing some momentous equator-like threshold, I was terrified, engulfed, laid waste by the vastness of the experience. I had to walk slowly in order to give the environment time. I could at best make out only bits, for the whole was unseizable, unreachable, everywhere and in all directions simultaneously. Each building had its version of the story, each wanted its say. By the side of a warehouse there stood a paddy field, next to that a fire station, next to that a shrine, next to that an apartment block – the laws of neat segregation and zoning of a place like London were obviously not in operation – the principle urban condition was collage. The totality of the city before me was indivisible from its constituent parts, whereas in London it had always been clear which was part, which was whole. There was no way of declaring, 'This is Tokyo', but rather, 'This plus this plus this are Tokyo', or more simply, 'Tokyo is the sum of all things from nought to infinity'. As Yoshizaka puts it, 'One time igniting, the next extinguishing, Tokyo has put together new worlds one after another with a new method every time' . . . All I could make out was architecture everywhere, in excess, forever and everywhere, a profusion of architectures blossoming, blooming, throbbing, ripening, a universal burgeoning. I walked downhill, without a map, following odd and scaring impulses, following streets packed with bars, grocers, small workshops, repair shops, stores of every imaginable type.

Alien environment

I have gone to some lengths to describe my first few hours in the new Japanese environment, for the rest of my three and a half years stay was a period of intense activity aimed at explaining as best I could those very first few hours . . . Or, in other words, if one wants to realise how environmental our lives are (that is, to what extent our existence is architectural), all one has to do is live in a foreign environment. The environment then becomes overwhelming, bulky, very much present, imposing itself on one in a physical way that one rarely gets to experience in one's own country. One's environmental attenuation (the degree to which one is plugged into architecture) is suddenly increased a hundred-fold; before, in one's home environment, it had been on a more or less conventionalised, anaesthetised, unconscious level – living in an alien environment, one automatically is made conscious of just how exactly one's being is environmental. As an alien, the ontological nature of architecture is intensified; one acts out one's becoming: one works, one laughs and plays – the environmental accompaniment in all these cases is made more acute for the alien. The environment is omnipresent, following us everywhere . . . buildings stake out our claims wherever we may go: however, living in one's native environment, such aspects are pretty much invisible and constitute the taken-for-granted collectivity that the non-alien lives out. The mental maps that people carry around in their imagination have been shown to be full of inconsistencies, blind-spots, hesitancies and ambiguities. Just imagine the alien's mental map – drawing it would amount to an environmental rite. For the non-alien, the environment does have emotional poles, but for the alien it is a maelstrom . . . and this is particularly so with the new Japanese environment.

The new Japanese environment

So what is it then, this new Japanese environment? How best to characterise the way it seems to follow one with its eyes, how best to convey its sensual and exotic traits? How can we best appreciate its visual space, and its multi-perspective illusions? In some respects, there are certain things which will not surprise an architect from the West – for example, Kajima, one of the largest design and construction companies, was recently found guilty of large scale handouts to local authority officials. Another large architectural office, Nikken Sekkei, recently had a model of a theatre built which cost more than it would to build a real house. These paradoxes are familiar everywhere and hardly raise an eyebrow now. Other things easy to grasp include Kara Jūro's theatre group, moving from city to city, performing in a large red tent – one year it was erected from an old coal barge and during the show it was towed along a canal; others are, for example, communes dotted about Japan, either religiously based such as Ittoen, or politically based such as Yamagishi-kai, experimenting with ways around the architectural norms; yet another example is the way the Burakumin, Japan's 'invisible race', a minority group long discriminated against by majority society, have of late become politicised, and through the efforts of the Kaihō Dōmei (Buraku Liberation Front) many environmental and community projects have been accomplished, in Sakae Shi, Naniwa-ku (Osaka), etc: all such developments run parallel with recent concerns in the West in defusing the institutionalised environment, and are thus relatively easy to assess . . . For the major part, however, the environment remains in the group of monopoly capital, though often in disguise – for example, the way the old parts of Shinjuku (Tokyo) are being replaced with gargantuan department stores, inside which are floors modelled on the intimate patterns of the former streets; we must not be fooled. Yet not everyone is against this petrification of the urban milieu . . . In the last five years, several tower blocks have arisen from the bowels of Shinjuku, and have been greeted in the architectural press as examples of great urban sculpture and in the national press as symbols of the future-form of Japanese life. So well have these blocks captured the popular imagination, that they have been used in ways that the architects involved could never have imagined. I have seen them illustrated on calendars, as the setting for a good many television film dramas and gangster series, children's cartoons, as a setting for fashion models, in promotional campaigns for cameras as well as being

The Umeda complex, 1932 and
the completed Hankyu Umeda
Terminal, 1976.

The wedge-shaped building
beside the seventeen-storey
tower was demolished to make
way for the new Hankyu Cinema
Town. Each cityscape
component changes at its own
rate, resulting in a metropolitan
panorama of transformation

featured in the adverts and films of the financing and construction companies involved. These torrid blocks have become the definitive image of the glamour of the urbanisation process. What is interesting is that, through the sub-contracting system operated by the construction forms involved, such as Kajima, most of the men employed in the blocks' construction are from Sanya, a Tokyo ghetto of daily-labourers.

'It was history's wont to progress by granting the wishes of some and denying those of others. No matter how distressing the future might prove to be, it did not necessarily disappoint everyone.' '. . . history could not be advanced by human volition.' 'The trousers of politics were a sodden, wrinkled mess, but what did that matter?'

Politics?

Doubts such as these, voiced by the novelist Mishima, continue to haunt the Japanese architect. An incident I witnessed in an architect's office in Tokyo illustrates this. A girl photographer had arrived to snap him for a magazine; as the architect posed, he became both male (for he was an object of veneration for the girl), and female (for he stood there absolutely passive as she shot away). Such a ripe situation, replete with de Sade-like overtones, is perhaps every architect's most secret ambition, and we can understand the mechanism of the new Japanese environment more clearly if we bear this in mind. Community or social commitments pale into insignificance by the side of such a basic male essence – adulation by and subjugation of a beautiful girl. She turned up in guerrilla style, dressed to kill, and took him by storm. The architect was reckless, pink-faced and extravagant for the rest of the afternoon . . . what social ideal could reward him thus?

Faced with the workings of a political and economic system independent of his own existence, the architect in Japan resorts to a kind of aesthetic Russian roulette through the design of the single house; in this way he not only accords with contemporary conditions but with historical ones as well. 'It would seem fair to say that an upper-class Victorian Londoner would tend to be at once more shocked and more fascinated by slums than his counterpart in Meiji Tokyo. The Japanese have simply never been taken with either the strong sense of propriety or the morbid investigation into impropriety as the Victorians. It seems at any rate that despite considerable poverty in industrialising Tokyo, the concern over the slums by the middle-class was considerably less. There was concern, of course, beginning in the 1880s in a series of journalistic exposés . . . Yet the Japanese reformers never produced studies as monumental as those of Mayhew and Booth . . . one index of the less Japanese preoccupation with the urban poor is the lack of any word as expressive as "slums" ' (l) Morse, writing in 1886, had this to say . . . 'the idea of cooperative buildings, with the exception of the Yashiki barracks, has never entered the Japanese mind, each family, with few exceptions, managing to have a house of its own.'

Cabaret

But still, these are global issues, not specifically Japanese. In order to get to what might provisionally be called the distinct character of the new Japanese environment, one must follow a different tack . . . for example, all one has to do is to walk into a big cabaret to hit this new environment head-on. Take, for instance, the Parco, in Namba, (S. Osaka) . . . one enters down a long escalator into the lobby where the hostesses are lined up, waiting. Some of them are in immaculate *kimonos*, while the rest are wearing gowns and dresses that would not have been out of place at an early fifties deb's ball. Officials, clean-cut and sharply dressed, stand ready for anything. From the top of the escalator one commands a view of the whole proceedings – entrance, lobby, then the mammoth entertainments space with the customer's cubicles in front of the stage . . . one feels as though one has entered a rather expensive and sickly cream cake. The guest arrives, is greeted by an immaculately groomed assistant, who then introduces the new arrival to the hostess first in the queue, unless he is a regular, in which case he has his regular girl – if she is otherwise engaged, he would be introduced to one of the newer girls. Then the couple are led to a vacant booth, from where they can see the floor-show. Drinks and snacks follow in rapid and expensive succession . . . The gigantic space, completed just the year before, has not a single flaw, has not a single thing out of place, as though obeying some pre-ordained order. The dizzying perspective of booths, stage, couples, the sordid textures to the materials, the electric ejaculations from the musicians create an undeniably unique space. What catches one's attention immediately is the homogeneity of men and women; usually at a dance, a party or any social event, there is always an imbalance, sometimes more men, sometimes more women and there is also the tendency for groups to gather, either all male or all female. But here, the male/female distribution was exactly even as though a highly ingenious machine had been run across the floor to achieve such an impartial ratio.

Other 'cabalets' (sic) in Osaka have to be seen to be believed, such as the Crown Shiko, built some fifteen years before, featuring 150 girls of average age about thirty, or the slightly more recent Monte Carlo, with a more modest 120 girls; a pink space, as though it had all been dusted with talcum powder, decorated with tinsel trees that rise up towards the chandeliered heavens. Some customers go every night; it has been found that they patronise a cabaret that regularly for about six months, when they would usually switch their allegiance to another. Customers who frequent the same establishment for about two or three nights a week would keep that up for about four years before changing. 1972 was the boom year when customers went to three or four in the same night, but now they tend to go to one or two instead. The customer might spend between Y10000 and Y15000 in one cabaret; hostesses' earnings for the real professional come to about Y1 million a month, while the less experienced could expect about Y150 000. (£1 = Y400.) It is up to the hostess herself what form the relationship takes when the cabaret ends at eleven. We must conclude our first glimpse of the frenetic urban surrealism so typical of the new Japanese environment by returning to the Crown Shiko . . . A solitary and youngish man on the stage plays muzak with an expressionless face; I suppose he realises that not a single customer comes to the cabaret to hear his electric-organ fantasies . . . their fantasies are elsewhere . . . Spot-lit above him – a plaster reproduction of a classical nude torso – perhaps it's the centre of some esoteric rites just before closing-time? The atmosphere is one of sinking, drowning, of being swallowed alive.

New-nature, new-luxury

Again, to discover the new Japan-as-architecture, all one has to do is to descend into one of the large underground shopping precincts to find one has let oneself in for more than one bargained for. One enters a world of rainbows projected onto fountains, plastic swans following eternally fixed paths in idyllic pools, waterfalls of staggering height . . . You may not exactly take to the massive fifteen metre stained glass 'window' or the illuminated landscape murals that change with the seasons, or the revolving Renaissance statuary, but the mechanised swan lazily following its circular course will almost fool you into thinking it will snap should you get too close. The form is interior, on multiple levels of dislocation reaching down into the cthonic depths. This particular version of the future is fixed, a synthetic environment that cannot be challenged – this new-nature is nothing more than the spectacle of man overtaken by his appetites. It symbolises the way architecture can obscure the real relations between man and environment through being transformed into a spectacle. An associated phenomenon is the new-luxury that is a vivid aspect of everyday urban life. Department stores, bars, tea and coffee-houses, restaurants and shopping-centres as well as hotel lobbies all receive the same treatment – ostentatious materials, marble floors, chrome fittings. These elements are used to create a universe so polished and shining one can hardly put a name to it – on entering such a space, we think ourselves guests of a specially beneficent deity whose gleaming palace we are free to walk through like heroes of some legend. (2)

Pachinko

One does not have to walk far in any Japanese town before one comes across a *pachinko* (pinball) 'hall' or 'parlour': what is surprising is that they are not restricted to a special entertainments area but are found everywhere. The interior is a confection of lacy trimmings, hectic wallpapers, plastic bouquets, chandeliers and endless mirror reflections. Initially, the decor was very simple, but that was quickly superseded by painted murals which were in turn outmoded by illuminated panels, and now kinetic perspex constructions are the vogue. The machine is a collage of reflections and sensations, becoming a neon mandala by means of which the player can free himself from the fetters of space and time. Development of this post-war phenomenon continues at break-neck speed, and the first hall of the next generation has already been built – the entrance hall is sheathed in travertine, a bronze elephant and some Greek sculptures flank the door, while the stuffed head of an ox is prominently on display above the marble wash-basin. The complex includes a T.V. lounge, a prize supermarket, computer-controlled machines and a choice of either Western or Japanese seating arrangements – all sections being escalator linked. The machines have earphones offering a choice of music, so that the player can be entirely removed from the real world and thus enter more fully into his own 'private future'.

The love-hotel;
Exterior
This building form contributes bodily to the trompe l'oeil cityscape. Eighth century Manyoshu poems speak of 'Pleasure Palace', and by the eighteenth century the 'amorous quarter' was integral to any Japanese town. The form might have changed, but not the content

Illusion and technology-as-toy

In an environment given over to the more or less free play of capital, a greater part of the environment's function is the manufacture of dreams and illusions to act as safety valves protecting that capital. There are *turko* (turkish baths) where the male guest can obtain a wide range of service from the masseuses – one *turko* has its girls dressed in schoolgirl uniform, while another is designed like a convent, whose girls, dressed as nuns, pray before a cross prior to work. There are private *kissatens* (coffee-houses) with individual and private cubicles which can be hired by couples by the hour . . . as well as the already well-known Love-hotels . . . This innate tendency to illusion spreads even to housing where *tate-uri* and *ikodate-jutaku*, the most prevalent forms of private housing provision of the past decade, are tarted up with tricks and devices not so different from the Love-hotels. (3) Still, illusion on an environmental scale is not peculiar to Japan – (there are more 'Greek' buildings in the U.S. than there are in Greece), it is just that in Japan it is done with so much enthusiasm, and is partly ascribable to the fact that technology has not been able to meet its promises and has thus been converted into a toy. In Shinkansen (the bullet train), the Japanese try to overtake the environment, leaving it behind in the gleaming wake of the fastest village-on-wheels in the world, but

of course it is impossible . . . the silk-smooth ride, the pneumatic hissing of automatic doors, the great precision with which component meets component – these might just fool one for the length of the journey; one only has to get out at one's destination for reality to strike . . .

Faced with a past that perhaps no longer belongs to them, they have invented a new Japanese environment as a spurious future, a kind of non-stop urban mirage. The corporate institutions exclude the individual by depriving him of meaning – they leave only gaps in their structures to be filled with private fantasy. Modern culture has no

Yōji Watanabe, Nishida House, Tokyo, 1966. Exterior
Alluding to Japanese castles, this bastion-like house could almost be mistaken for a love-hotel; there is the same super-scaled graphic exterior woven from over-literal quotes taken from history books, there is the same concealed entrance, modest planting, air of secrecy . . .

Toyokazu Watanabe,
Romanesque Momoyamadai,
Osaka, 1977
Exterior
This group of residences shares
certain stylistic affinities with the
love-hotel, but is more ironically
explicit in doing so than Yōji
Watanabe's Nishida House. The
architect explains . . . 'This is an
assembly of terrace houses for
sale in lots in Senri-New-Town.
Generally speaking, Japanese like
'style', and by appealing to it we
try to get people to buy. The
relation between the designer
and the buyer is similar to that
of the tradition of Japanese
accomplishments like Kabuki.'

place for the man it created. He must find a place outside his own era in nostalgia or utopia. The illusion of the new Japanese environment gives the individual a chance to escape through the gaps to find private meanings not normally available. But the illusion is enclosed within the real world. It can appear an independent, privileged, elevated sanctuary only with the help of self delusion on the part of anyone who might enter it. The illusion 'is a mirror which makes beautiful that which is distorted' (Shelley). The illusion tries to give to the environment a vision-like quality – one experiences a sudden rush of visual adrenalin, such as when entering the Mitsukoshi department store in Hirakata Shi; the walls either side of the escalator 'up' are faced with mirrors, so one rises accompanied by an infinity of reflections following one's diagonal course. One enters a fairy-tale wonderland where anything is possible as long as one does not think twice.

Air conditioned temples

Perhaps the building type that has most strikingly assimilated these phenomenological vectors is the new religions' temple or H.Q. . . . Since the last war, many of these sects have enjoyed considerable success, most ostensible being the meteoric rise to pre-eminence of Sōka Gakkai under the charismatic and photogenic leader, Daisaku Ikeda. The new religions' centres create environments of optimistic promise and mystical titillation: often the plan is circular, as is the case with Seicho-no-Ie's main shrine, focusing on their fascist symbol, as is also the case with the Great Sacred Hall, of Risshō-Kōsei-Kai. Sometimes the H.Q. becomes a city in itself – witness the new Buddhist city at Tenri-shi, or the mixture of the sacred and Disneyland in P.L. Land, Perfect Liberty's H.Q. south of Osaka. The most carefully orchestrated of these, however, undoubtedly belongs to Sōka Gakkai's centre at Taisekiji, nestling under the soaring peak of Mt. Fuji . . . Shō Hondo, the recently completed main shrine is the climax of a long pilgrimage route through the complex. One enters the Garden of Law, and passes through the massive Pavilion of Perfect Harmony before reaching the epicentre of Shō Hondo, the fully air-conditioned Mystic Sanctuary, into which only members are allowed. It amounts to an all-out assault on one's senses, an unending psychodrama of light and dark, a religious expo. This kind of architecture dissolves contradictions and restores to the believer a unitary world in which demands are in accordance with facts, in which everything reaches a metaphysical equilibrium normally denied by the ordinary environment. The believer experiences a feeling of mastery over and lucidity towards the menacing world because the architecture provides him with a solution for all threats and a posture to assume in the face of them. (4)

Archaic roots and correspondences

Initially, I conceived of these 'techniques-of-ecstasy' as being a particular feature of the new environment, but the more I came into contact with the archaic environment, through visiting *matsuri* (festivals) and old shrines and temples, the more I came to realise that in these religious and ritual techniques we can discover the point of

Ueno City, Oni Matsuri (Demon Festival), October 23–5
Annual expulsion of 'demons' to protect the city for the forthcoming year

Cave – Shrine, Zen-Arai-Benten, Kamakura
The busy atmosphere and lavish decorations aren't so very different from that of a Tokyo store . . . add the fact that the shrine is devoted to the deity of prosperity and that people bring money there to purify by washing, and we have doubly strong correspondence between the archaic and the new

Kyoto, Jizo-O-Bon, August 23
Annual children's festival

Himeji, Kenka Matsuri (Fight Festival), October 15
Annual festive trial of strength – the community whose *mikoshi* (palanquin) survives the battering will enjoy a year's prosperity

Kobe, Ikuta Matsuri, April 15–16
Annual commemoration of the Ikuta Shrine's foundation – the photo shows the procession winding its way through a local school

departure for many of the new environment's ecstatic elements. One striking resemblance is between *matsuri* processions and student marches . . . Pachinko, too, has archaic precedents, when one considers the number of games one can find in temple compounds and when one remembers the sacred significance games of chance have for the primitive . . . the atmosphere of a pachinko hall, by only a little stretch of the imagination, corresponds quite closely to a Buddhist meditation hall. The phenomenal speed of renewal of the new Japanese environment, as dramatised by Metabolism, is related closely to the annual renewal of ritual objects during the *matsuri* and the periodic rebuilding of shrines, Ise in particular. Cave-shrines might be thought of as the beginning of the great underground complexes in the main cities, and in the shrines propped up on mountain sides, for example Sanbutsuji, we can recognise precedents for many of the structural gambits in the new environment.

Either one looks on Japanese history as one long fashion parade, or else as a link between the present and some deep past instant . . . I tend to go along with the latter, which leads me to regard these new techniques-of-ecstasy as not so different from the ritual technologies embodied in Shinto and Buddhist practices. In the house, especially, we can trace this continuity from the archaic to the present . . .

(*scenario*):   one day, Tange, having hid a knife up his sleeve, said to a young architect, 'I hear you understand what the Japanese house really is; is that so?' The young architect replied, 'It is so.' Tange said, 'What is the Japanese house?' The young architect stuck up his finger and Tange cut it off with the knife. As the young architect ran out in tears, Tange called out and said, 'What is the Japanese house?' The young architect, lifting up his hand (to stick out his finger) saw no finger there and became suddenly enlightened.

CHAPTER TWO

HOUSE/HOME

Sumeba miyako.
. . . house, houseboat, housebreaker, housecoat, household, housekeeper, houseless, houseman, house of cards, housewarming, housetop, house-trained, housewife, housework, housing, mad-house, to be out of house and home, the house of the rising sun, house to house . . . home, at home, home-coming, homefolks, home ground, home-keeping, homeland, homeless, home-life, homely, home-made, home rule, homesick, homespun, home-stead, home-truth, homeward-bound, homework, homing, home-team, home-crowd, home-run, home-counties, home on the range, holiday-home, broken-home, homey . . .

Having described the new environment, we have posited one context from which the new Japanese house acquires meaning. Another, equally important, is the general nature of the house, a personal reading of which guides the architect during the design and realisation process. The special characteristics of the new Japanese house is that it is the product of a collision between an ecstatic technology and certain bedrock axioms regarding 'house'.

The house: one enters, and is welcomed, by one's children, one's parents, one's wife, one's mistress, one's grandparents, whoever. One enters a yolk-like zone, all centre, and cannot withstand its magnetic feelers. One is greeted by memories, which come running up, several at a time, jumping into one's arms. One enters in much the same way a cat seeks out the point of optimal comfort on someone's lap. One has no control over these sensations, one must submit to the radii leading to the hub. Whether it be a crow making its nest in the stomach of a dead man (one of Mozuna's primary images of dwelling space) or a schizophrenic making a hideout, it amounts to the same thing: house. There is no way of avoiding it – it permeates the environment at all levels, so much so that we conceive of the environment as a hierarchy of houses.

Dream-house

Dōdeskaden, a film by Akira Kurosawa, is about the dreams and illusions of a derelict community. The main character is a boy who thinks himself a tram-driver – every day, from morning to night, he goes back and forth along his 'route' through the community, stopping to pick up passengers, calling out 'Dōdeskaden, Dōdeskaden', the sound the

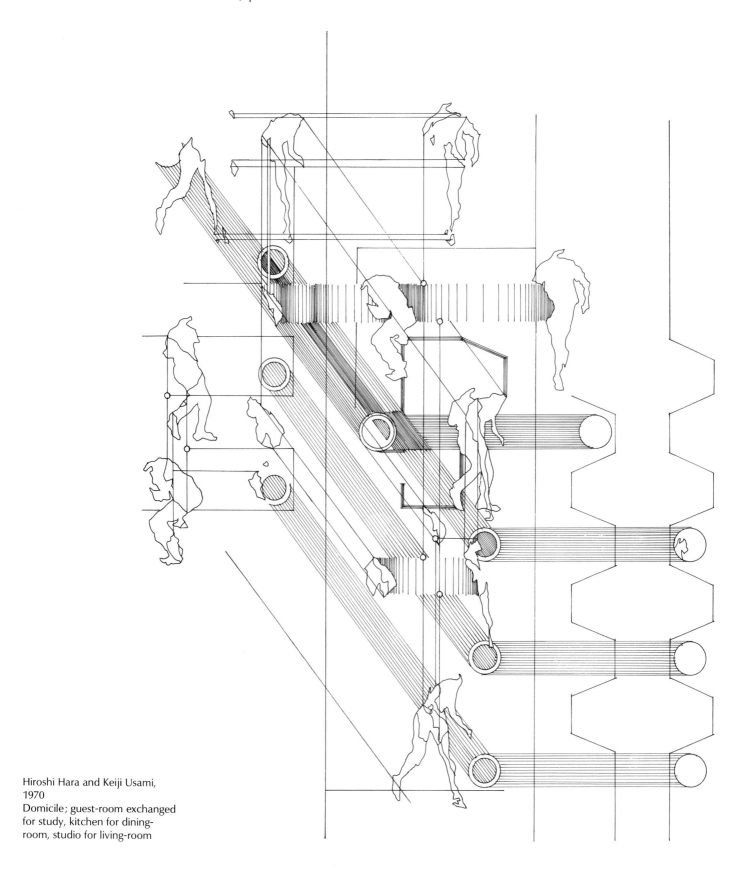

Hiroshi Hara and Keiji Usami,
1970
Domicile; guest-room exchanged
for study, kitchen for dining-
room, studio for living-room

Chris Fawcett, A House In The City
Sectional Axonometric
Lower levels comprising a hotel are topped by a residential roofscape – house-as-attic; the hotel, in its provision of anonymous private cells on the one hand and public lobby space on the other, falls exactly midway between 'house' and 'city'. The complex density of programme is an emblem of Tokyo itself, concentration – city

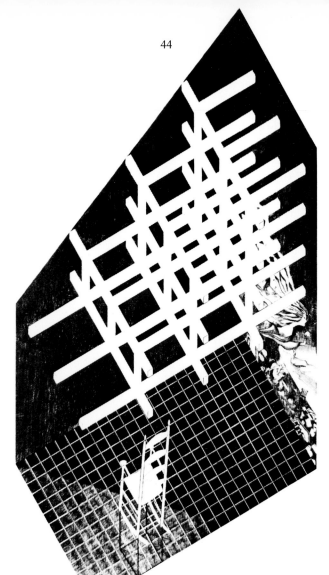

Submitted to the Shinkenchiku Residential Competition judged by James Stirling

Tomotsune Honda; dream image of bedroom and dining-room

tram makes. Living in an abandoned car in the same community is a tramp in his late twenties and a young boy. The tramp spends all his time describing to the boy the house they were going to live in when their luck changed . . . he begins with a gate, and considers the various styles he might have (all of them flashed on the screen) – Classical, Rococo, Spanish, and he turns over in his mind the different colour permutations open to him. He decides on an imposing Florentine style, one with a white painted perimeter wall of Baroque pretensions. Next he conjures up the house, and after a lot of very careful consideration he opts for a modern, metal panel asymmetrical structure, with flying terraces and roof-gardens, finally deciding on a flaky red lustre. The windows were of generous size, with billowing lace curtains fit for a princess . . .

This introduces one of the main aspects of the house that I shall deal with here – the intimate entente between house and dream; others I shall discuss include – the house as a settling-in-the-earth, the house-as-dwelling, concluding with an introduction to the sacred components of the house, which will be dealt with more comprehensively in the next chapter. The house can be defined in highly diverse ways – for example, as the place where suicide is most likely to occur; an alternative definition could be derived

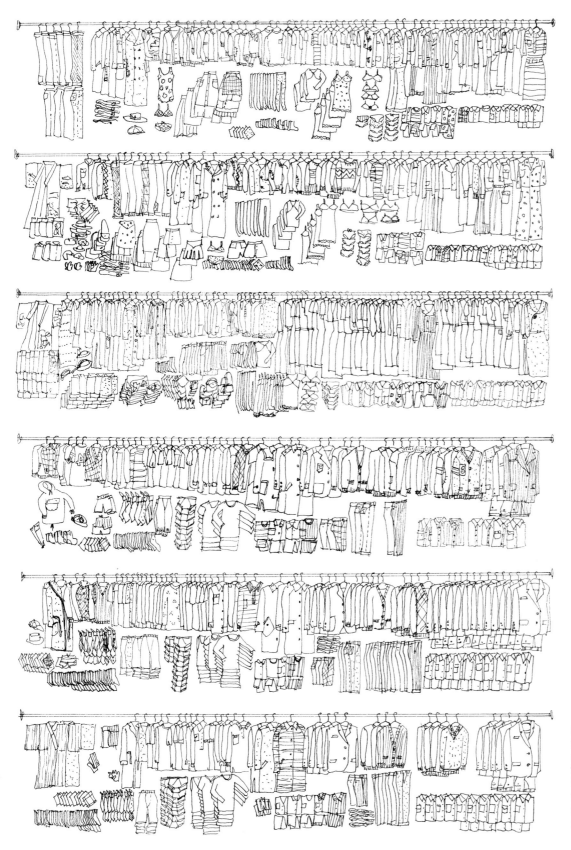

Six people volunteered to have
their wardrobe contents
surveyed by Takashi Kurosawa
for the magazine *Toshi-Jutaku*
(*Urban Housing*); the resultant
treasure troves of possessions
the survey revealed point to the
museum role played by house

			god			
			house			
			man			
heaven	house	earth		primitive	house	urban
			self			
			house			
			true self			

			out			
			house			
			in			
death	house	life		being	house	becoming
			idiosy–ncracy			
			house			
			archetype			

The transformational nature of house

from the fact that on long car journeys, most accidents happen within the vicinity of home. More often, the house is portrayed as a point of definition in the unlimited extent of the environment, a point where many factors join together; the household, owing to this coalescing, is the original political unit. The house-as-a-point-of-definition is fundamental to its territorial nature – viz. the way it stakes out a place and demarcates its possession, marking off 'mine' from 'others'. Hence it makes the environment as a whole tolerable by providing an escape route, however temporary . . . This home-forming-tendency was thought of as Teutonic, but it is universal . . . An experiment was carried out in the U.S. with someone living in a cave for six months. A tent was provided as a place for sleeping and providing a hub or refuge from the ill-defined space of the cave, though the cave's environment was ideal in terms of temperature, humidity, etc, for a house . . .

'. . . the eyes live in the world, just as man dwells in a house . . .' (1)

Existence house

The house is a plane on which our existence is inscribed. The house is the beginning and the end of architecture; it will be found at both ends of the spectrum. It has a dual character, one externally fixed, the other infinitely manipulable; the fixed aspect denotes 'house', the adjustable aspect connoting 'mine'. When one feels tossed about by uncertainties and anxieties, the house is indeed reassuring, with its ceremonies, its mysteries and its archaic credentials. As children, we play at building house: in ritual too, houses are built – often models act as substitutes today. Marriage usually entails moving to a new or different house, and in some languages, as in Thai, to marry is called 'to have a house' (2) (*mi-ruan*). The kings of Egypt were called *per-aa* (Pharaoh), 'The Great House' (3), much as we say, 'the White House today announced . . .'. In other words, the house phenomenon has unleashed yet other phenomena . . . when taking photos of architectural patterns on summer clothes ('How to Wear Architecture'), I found that the building type that figured most was the house, just as house images predominate in the secondary environment, that constituted by the mass media. The house is such a universally diffused thing that one could devote a long time trying to reckon it up; the magic houses in fun-fairs, the fact that the average American moves fourteen times in his life, a Briton eight times, a Japanese five times (I have already moved more than twenty times), the haunted house, the church as the 'House of God' . . . These are some of the areas, randomly taken, that might figure in such a reckoning.

World house

We tend to subdivide the world into small manageable bits, and label each 'house'; this affords us occasional respite from the drudgery of labour, we can dawdle, tarry, and allow our minds free play. The speculative ability developed out of our ability to dwell. We divided the entire space/time project into twelve astrological houses, the democratic machinery into the House of Commons and the House of Lords, and the city is increasingly being sub-divided into 'house' – every new office block comes to be christened 'Metropolis House', 'City Gate House', 'Mercantile House'; high rise flats, factories, shops – all 'house'. Showing some photos of modern buildings to pre-literate Lahu shifting cultivators in their North Thai mountain village, every building type I showed them they took to be a house, whether it were a multi-rise mirrored glass office block, or indeed an actual house, by Richard Meier for example. Their own village comprised houses alone, and it was the model for their understanding of the world as a whole. The Japanese form of geomancy is called '*kaso*', and is now used to determine the siting of any building, although originally, as its literal translation suggests ('house-structure'), it was formerly concerned solely with the location and disposition of houses. We enter the world via the house.

The memory of a house . . . . . . as a series of rooms in which one had at one time or another slept; while the unseen walls kept changing, adapting themselves to the shape of each successive room remembered, whirling madly through the darkness . . .' (4).

On a hot beach, the way a dog will dig up cool sand to lay on, that is home. In the game of hide and seek, hiding is home, as is scrambling into the cupboard under the stairs when a storm breaks. How is it that houses started to be given names . . . in England this is common, in Japan very rare . . . the house called 'home' in the film 'Clockwork Orange' is a case in point. Home is where one can pick one's nose best; more politely put, one sustains a home by a sort of continuous creation – it becomes one's own by a process of perpetual renewal. The calm loyalty of one's possessions revealing no surprises, could be the basic definition of home that these sentences are

Kumiko Shimada, 'World House'
The architect comments; 'Mud
huts covering the hills of Kabul,
an old Greek monastery,
wooden houses at the back of
the Blue Mosque, Italian hillside
towns – all mixed up, looking for
a nationality – isn't this what
makes these look like modern
Japanese houses?'

searching out for. Home offers pure interiority safe from the vicissitudes and contingencies of an outside world of pure exteriority . . . a man returns home and removes his tie, a woman changes her bra.

'It began to rain much more heavily. It bucketed down on the black back-yard and the little comfy kennel of a house.' (5).

Without house

It is a paradox of our times that the more 'homeless' we feel, the more elaborately do we build houses, little realising that home and house are not one and the same thing. 'Most Americans are not at home in their land.' (6) Having to defend one's house with a gun; obviously one cannot feel at home in such circumstances – one tries to fill the house with a weight of furnishings and thereby stem this outflowing of home. Homelessness has always been a vivid fear stalking man, as expressed in Thomas Wolfe's *You Can't Go Home Again*. To be homeless usually means being a social outcast, a being discriminated against and despised for living like an animal. This has subtle variations – a town Shikuramachi, Chiba province, was surveyed and all houses were found to have a four-room arrangement (*yotsuma*). Those houses without such an arrangement were not considered 'homes' and their occupants considered outsiders. But sometimes, being out of house and home can have a positive meaning . . . 'It is clear that, as taught by the Buddha, salvation is best attainable by those of the homeless, bhikka state . . .'. (7) In Japan, to become a monk is '*shukke*', to leave home. In other words, to be homeless can mean to have transcended all material needs and to have reached an incomparably superior mental state. In fact, some cultures in the world manage quite well without houses – the Mrabri, a North Thai hill-tribe have no houses – home for them is a hearth. But not everyone can manage so easily – imagine a homeless family in England being told that their condition was as a result very spiritual and enviable – I imagine they would react much in the same way as if they had gone to apply for somewhere to live and been given the word 'house' in reply. Some souls of the dead, in Japan, are considered 'homeless', that is they cannot find the way back to their former dwellings, and offerings of food are made to them on the *kamidana* (see below); this practice has the latent effect of reinforcing the sense of home among the members of the household making such an offering.

'Systematic studies reveal that . . . when an area is evacuated (after a disaster), the majority of the inhabitants do not leave. Those who do flee are primarily transients and tourists – not the people who live there.' (8)

Roof house

One of the ploys used in the traditional Japanese house to mitigate against an intrusion of homelessness is to top off the living space with a huge mountain-roof; so much so that one might be tempted to think of the Japanese house as a roof, while the thatch invariably reminds one of nesting material. We should not be surprised then to learn that '*su*' in '*sumu*' (to live) means in fact 'nest'. The character 家 (*ie ya, uchi*; house),

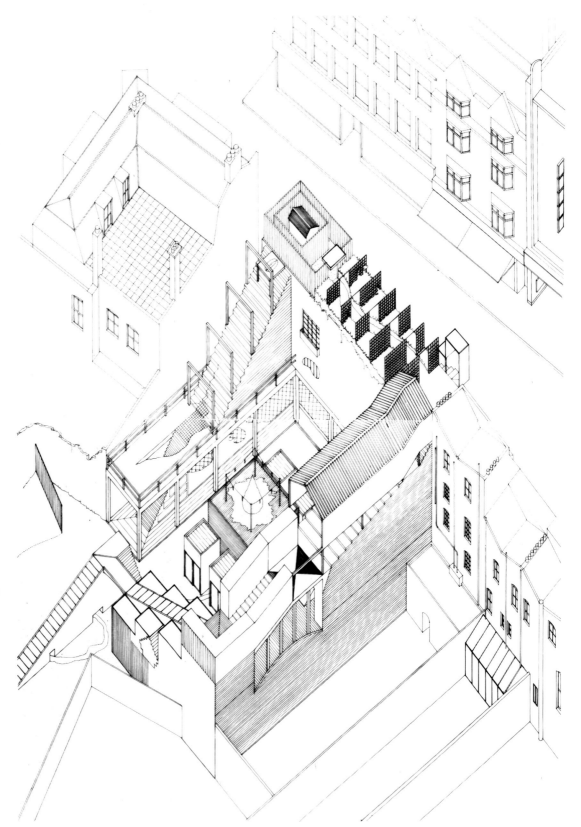

Chris Fawcett, House, No-House
Axonometric
This design attempts to
summarise Japanese notions of
'homelessness'. On the one
hand, being without house is
thought of as almost a
prerequisite of creativity – the
great poets have composed on
long journeys away from home
and wandering teacher/priests
have been vital in the
dissemination of new ideas. But
on the other hand, being
without a house in Japan City is
viewed as something
contemptible and not the
responsibility of the authorities

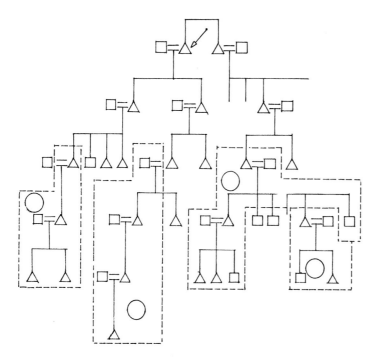
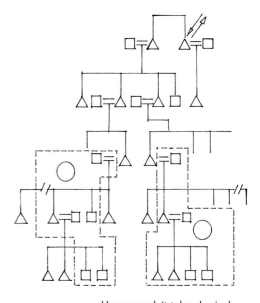

House needn't take physical form – the Japanese for house, 'ie', also means 'family', and 'kin'. These genealogical charts, taken from a Japanese village, describe 'house' as well as anything. The resemblance between these charts and the plan of Katsura can be no accident

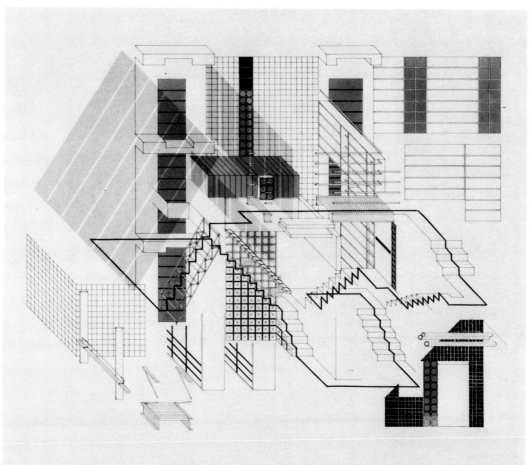

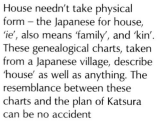

Akira Komiyama, House Project 3
Particularising house – shaping house from out of its intrinsic material details rather than trying to begin from a generalisation

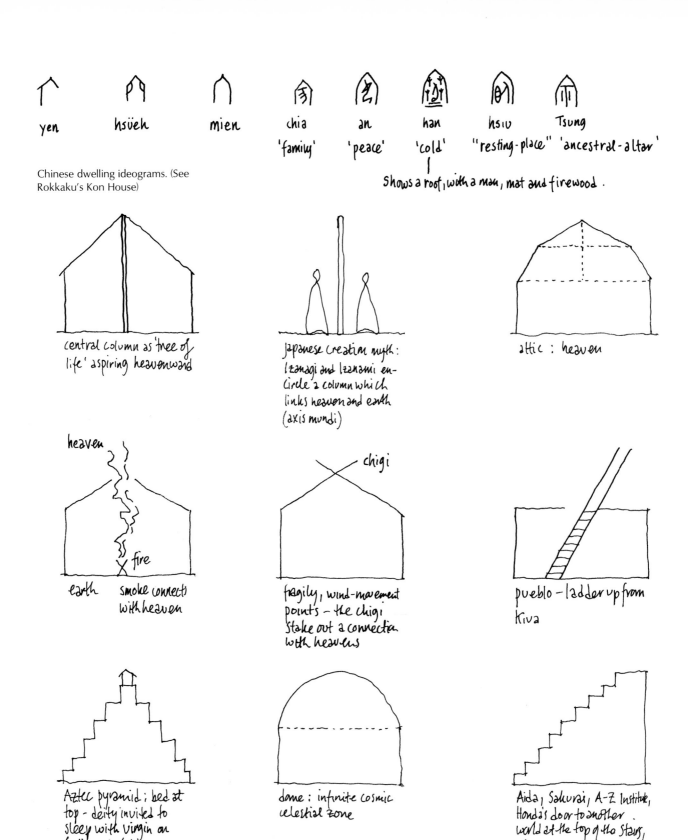

yen

hsüeh

mien

chia
'family'

an
'peace'

han
'cold'

hsiu
"resting-place"

Tsung
'ancestral-altar'

Chinese dwelling ideograms. (See Rokkaku's Kon House)

Shows a roof, with a man, mat and firewood.

central column as 'tree of life' aspiring heavenward

Japanese creation myth: Izanagi and Izanami encircle a column which links heaven and earth (axis mundi)

attic : heaven

heaven

fire

earth   smoke connects with heaven

chigi

fragily, wind-movement points – the chigi stake out a connection with heavens

pueblo – ladder up from kiva

Aztec pyramid; bed at top – deity invited to sleep with virgin on festive night

dome : infinite cosmic celestial zone

Aida, Sakurai, A-Z Institute, Honda's door to another world at the top of the stairs, etc...

House as threshold

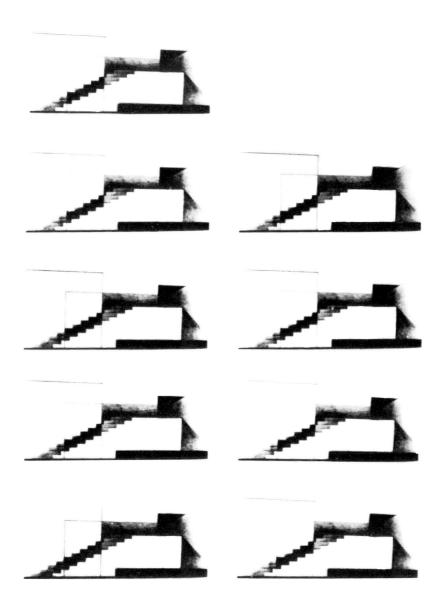

Kiyoshi Sakurai, Image of parents' house
His father is confined to a wheelchair; the heroization of the house as a heavenward-bound flight of steps takes on an unreal complexion in this light

represents a pig beneath the roof of a house, owing to the customary cohabitation of man and his domestic animals. The roof is also stressed in the original Chinese ideographic language from which Japanese is derived. There are three main radicals (components of ideographs) which have to do with dwellings; *yen*, which must have originally depicted a lean-to shelter against a cliff; *hsüeh*, which was originally a drawing of a cave or pit-dwelling; and *mien*, which is frankly a roof. From these origins derive the greater number of characters concerning house types and parts. (9) 'A roof tells its *raison d'être* right away; it gives mankind shelter from the rain and sun he fears. Geographers are constantly reminding us that, in every country, the slope of the roof is the surest indication of climate. We "understand" the slant of a roof . . . Up near the roof all our thoughts are clear. In the attic it is a pleasure to see the bare rafters of the strong

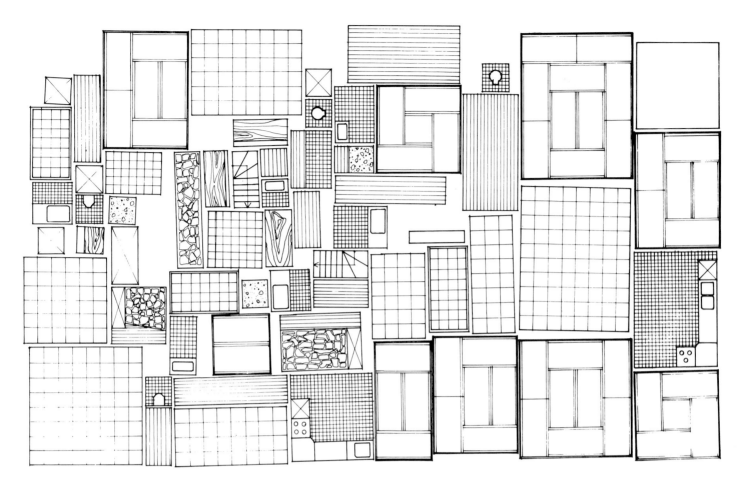

Tony Barter, 'Japanese House'
Should a couple wish to have a
house built, they can try out
alternative layouts by
rearranging the parts of a kit
they can buy in any downtown
store. The pack includes a
compass and geomantic
diagrams so that the house can
be sited auspiciously. Tony
Barter's 'house' is an aleatoric
configuration of the parts

framework. Here we participate in the carpenter's strong geometry.' (10) 'Should not every apartment in which man dwells be lofty enough to create some obscurity overhead, where flickering shadows may play about the rafters?' (11) This emphasis on the roof is also part of a larger system of interactions in which the house can be seen as a threshold between heaven and earth; the house today is where attic and basement meet, the attic reminding us of the heavens, the basement recalling the earth; such a division is a very old one, corresponding to the upper part of a Chinese house being considered Yang while the lower part was Yin.

Ontological house

'In the superficially empty house
There is no family, then it is more
Painful than on a journey.' (Manyoshu, no. 376)
(If there is no-one at home, then it is more distressing than the hostels (*yadori*) one stays at during a journey. *Yadori* literally means 'temporary house'.)

The ontological status of the Japanese house, hinted at in the title, can be found in the fact that the root '*i*' in '*ie*' (house) denotes not only 'to live' but also 'to be' – hence the house is very much bound up with one's existence, with one's being-in-the-world. A corollary of this is that with the termination of one's existence the house, too, comes to an end. Certainly it is this accommodation of the temporary nature of the house and its inevitable kinship with death that distinguishes the Chino–Japanese tradition. For Chinese scholars, life was a brief sojourn and their houses were correspondingly simple and rudely constructed. When the great general Liu Piu proposed to build a new house as a gift for a venerable scholar, the offer was persistently declined. (12) For the ordinary Christian, home suggested security, familiarity and *permanence* (13), although for the Puritans the earth was only a temporary abode – their true home was their father's house, which was in heaven. (The heavenly home has now been reduced to a well-serviced split-level in suburbia.) In Japan, an art of 'insecurity' bloomed, glorifying the transient and the fleeting, best embodied in Hōjōki, a diary of a thirteenth century hermit who built his own hut high up in the mountains. The book opens powerfully on this note – 'Ceaselessly the river flows, and yet the water is never the same, while in the still pools the shifting foam gathers and is gone, never staying for a moment. Even so is man and his habitation.' (14) Throughout the piece the same theme is reiterated . . . 'And who knows . . . why with so much labour he builds his house?' To emphasise the impermanent nature of his hut, he declares that he did not take the usual precaution of deciding the site by divination, as was the current practice. This is not the place to go into detail on the relationship between house and death, the logical outcome of the transience of man and building, all I can do is make a few hints – death is sometimes spoken of as 'going home', or as being 'at home with god'; houses are often built over graves; houses are sometimes built as offerings to the dead; coffins, too are sometimes house-shaped, for example the old Buddhist version in Japan . . . An entry by Suzokei Kenkyūshō in an architectural competition showed a *tatami* mat, marked with dots, which were annotated – 'This is the point where my brother died', 'This is the point where my sister died' . . .

" 'Why are they going away?' he asked, sitting down again. 'They would be just as comfortable here. Their house may be bombed the day they get back.'

'Yes', said Lola. 'But it's *their* house. Don't you understand that?'

'No.'

'Well, that's how it is. After a certain age one likes to meet trouble at home.' " (15)

Memory house

For Bachelard, the house is an automatic mechanism that triggers off a chain of associations and memories. A sort of attraction for images concentrates them about the house. The house is the germ of the essential, the original shell, the chosen spot, a cradle, a root in the corner of the world; but these are not characteristics of the house alone – all really inhabited space becomes home. Through dreams, odd recollections, chance events, the various dwellings in our lives co-penetrate, retaining the treasures of former days, exhibiting all the psychological elasticity of an image that moves us at an unimaginable depth. Life begins in the bosom of the house; the house we were born in is the house we will always live in; I asked a group of students of architecture at Kyoto University to sketch and describe the house they were born in – the depth of things

Shin Takamatsu, Komakine House, 1976–7
The architect has written . . . 'Don't stop the funeral processions, which, never reaching the gravepost of matter, are repeated with the sorrow of forfeiture and with its pleasures too.'

Toyokazu Watanabe, Nakano House, 1979
The architect admits that he had in mind the traditional Japanese gravestone during the course of designing this house for a painter

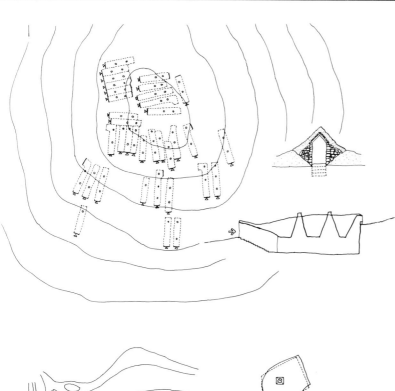

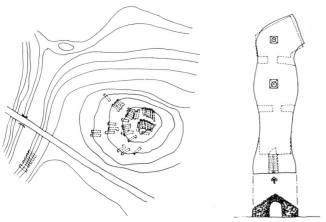

Tomotsune Honda and Yasunori Yada, survey of Calcavodo del Paran
Underground dwellings – the house-as-cave is an important ingredient in any dwelling – in the cupboard under the stairs, in the shadowy recesses and alcoves as well as the cellars and lofts. This type of survey technique is common among Japanese architects – Hiroshi Hara's series of monographs surveying world village types is perhaps the most comprehensive. Makoto Suzuki's analyses of Alpine Villages, Mayumi Miyawaki's appraisals of Japanese Temple approach routes, Yuichiro Kojiro's work on the architectural space of communities and their festivals are representative. Kon Wajiro, at the turn of the century, wandered from village to village, minutely documenting their houses, utensils, etc; this has been acknowledged as an exemplar

stirred up by such a project is very profound . . . that house will forever remain the definitive house, that by which all other houses across the environment will be measured. The cellar is 'the dark entity' of the house, it becomes 'buried madness, walled-in tragedy', while the stairs allow for a bit of heroism. What kind of house would Bachelard have built?

'Society provides us with warm, reasonably comfortable caves in which we huddle with our fellows, beating on the drums that drown out the howling of the surrounding darkness. "Ecstasy" is the act of stepping outside the caves to face the night, alone.' (16)

Settling house

According to Thoreau, who did actually build, a house was a rest from a journey. The rest usually took place at night, and thus the dwelling was related to the heavens rather than the day and earth. Dwelling was a matter of settling-in, wedging ourselves in till we come to rock bottom . . . which we call reality . . . a place where a wall might be found. Thus dwelling entails establishing a rapport with geology. The hut he built himself at Walden he called 'a porch at the entrance to a burrow'. Dwelling means 'settling' that is a progressive and continuous act, never 'settled'. He called the clearings and woods around the house his 'best room', and declared that . . . 'it was I and fire that lived there . . .' In the end, however, he became 'settled', and sensing imminent stagnation, had to leave to resume his journey, leaving the hut to its fate – burrow becomes house becomes burrow. In the grand American tradition, house for him was a verb.

'Some were returning, going back to the places they had left . . . leaving in order to return. They go out to obtain walling material to make the thick walls of their houses thicker, stronger than ever to return to.' (17)

Thinking house

To reach Heidegger's position on this, one might go via Norberg-Schulz. In his opinion, the house brings us inside, and answers a basic need for 'being somewhere'. This is the essential function of dwelling, and the house remains the central place our paths repeatedly cross. The structure of the house is primarily an enclosed space containing a subordinate structure of existential foci and connecting paths. The fireplace is the very centre of the dwelling and the bed is another hub where man starts and ends his day. This just about brings us to Heidegger. Place for him is an act of assembling; dwelling is an act of place; building is the gathering together of men, materials and ideas with a view to dwelling. 'Spatialisation began with the clearing of a forest.' (18) This brings forward freedom and opening for the dwelling of man. Spatialisation – that is locating, situating, bringing forward a locality that speaks and shelters at one and the same time. The house should be a topology of being, with both dweller and builder as poet. A house as an in-stalling in the sheltering earth, in closest proximity to man's metabolism. He is interested in how architecture provides an opportunity for dwelling. He distinguishes between inhabiting and dwelling, and consequently he divides architecture into buildings and dwellings; thus we have –

```
verb              noun
to inhabit   →    building
to dwell     →    dwelling
```

Then he admits that the distinction between building and dwelling is not so great, and that it might be better to designate building as a means towards dwelling –

```
means             end
building     →     dwelling
```

Etymologically we can find a clue to the intimacy of the two terms, building and dwelling. *Bauen* is the Old English and High German word for building, while buan means to dwell; building = dwelling. He also counts *bauen* as one of the original forms of *bin*, 'to be', thus adding to our thesis with regard to the ontological nature of the house –

$$dwelling \quad = \quad being$$

Bauen also means to protect, care for, cultivate –

```
dwelling   =    building as cultivation
           =    building as construction
```

Thus he sketches out the phenomenology of the house as a correlate of dwelling, careful not to separate man and space too much.

'This space below my navel, my loins and legs down to the soles of my feet are in truth my original nature . . . This space below my navel is in truth my original home.' (19)

Sacred house

Of course, the house has sacred components too . . . the house is a flexible stage on which both profane and sacred actions are performed. For the primitive constructing his hut, he perceives his action as an act of participation with the environmental spirits or deities which animate the area in which he lives. To build is therefore to enter into an agreement with these deities, whom he must propitiate through offerings, ritual, and obeying certain taboos. With the completion of the hut, it is still considered to be a part of the environmental and sacred system, and often a house-god is enshrined there and entertained regularly through ritual. Other deities too are commonly found, for example god of the site, god of the path, god of the gates, god of the hearth, kitchen, etc, all of whom demand occasional tribute. This will be expanded in the next chapter. In Christian eyes, this is very pagan stuff, and they did their best to stamp it out, viewing the house as a place in which a family should live a model ethical life, creating a church-like home that the Mormons for example have recently begun to re-emphasise. Their members are exhorted to follow the Lord's house as a perfect model for their own home, and the ideal is a temple-like environment, an environment that can make their homes more like heaven on earth. Paul derives the sanctity of the home from the fact that it reflects the mysterious relationships which subsist within the very being of the

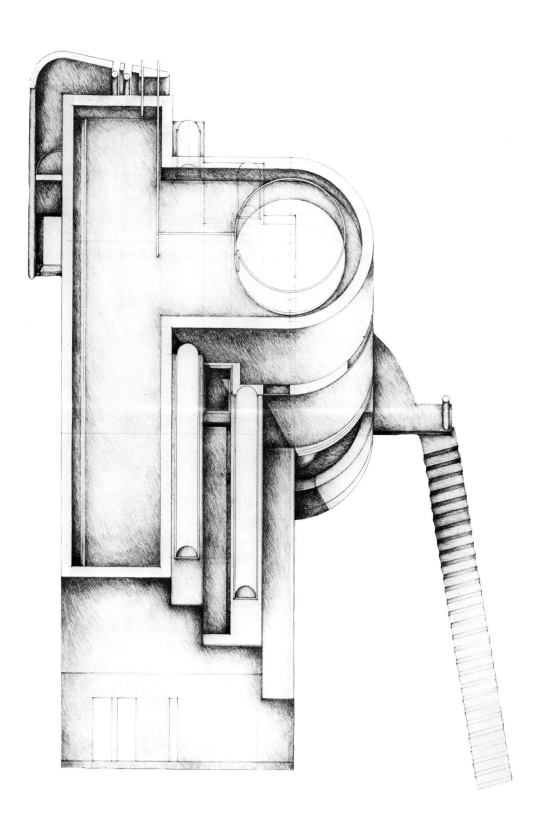

Shin Takamatsu, Komakine
House, Axonometric
The architect . . . 'I want to
memorise in my hand, now if
possible, that the first vestige of
architecture is in air cut by
matter.'

Minoru Takeyama, Living-room
1970

A Time/Space/Score for a
revitalised abode. 'In living
bodies, or phenomenal bodies,
existence, space and time always
agree.'

deity itself. Thoreau described the hut at Walden as fit to entertain a travelling god, while Heidegger considered dwelling as meaning respecting 'the fourfold nature of the world – the earth, the sky, the deities and mortals . . .' In Hōjōki, the recluse described his hut as the most rudimentary possible, but then one finds him saying, 'On the west is the shelf for the offerings of water and flowers to Buddha, and in the middle against the western wall is a picture of Amida Buddha . . .' Then these must have been considered 'bare necessities', 'absolute essentials' for someone so scalding about materialistic values. It is this sacred dimension I shall look at more anthropologically in the next chapter. The complexity of it can be hinted at briefly – for example, one of the Japanese names for shrine is 'miya', literally meaning 'august (noble) house'.

'Hindus have called it *moksha*, the absolute freedom. There is nothing like it. The whole prison is shattered. You are simply under the infinite sky. Fear grips you; you want to go back to your home, cosy, walled, fenced. The infinite is not there, you are not afraid.' (20)

There is a poem of Bashō's, on leaving his house for a long journey:

> Behind this door
> Now buried in deep grass
> A different generation will celebrate
> The Festival of Dolls. (21)

CHAPTER THREE

HOUSE/RITUAL

Kabe ni mimi ari, shoji ni me ari

The space of a house is activated by many ritual occasions. Birth, puberty, engagement, marriage, death – each of these occasions, and more, brings the ritual flexibility and suppleness into play, each of these ceremonies being elaborated differently according to the particular cultural milieu of kinship, economic and social patterns in which it is situated. I shall here initially confine myself to the *butsudan**, the *kamidana*† and the rituals involving them, in order to give a sketch of some of the relationships obtaining between house and ritual in Japan. Do not think that these two installations monopolise all domestic ritual – much is carried out without reference to them, but again this is not the time to go into them in detail, all I can do within the scope of these notes is indicate very roughly the Japanese house as a ceremonial field. The physical arrangement of the rooms and floor space carries social and ritual meanings, and through a ceremony these latter meanings are actualised. The scope of the house during ritual occasions becomes much more comprehensive, obliterating the normal restrictions of everyday life. Things normally tabooed are suddenly possible, things usually one way can be turned another – for example, when a death occurs in Japan, an ordinary folding screen is put around the dead body, but is put upside down, a powerful expression of death as an unexpected and serious lesion of normal relations. The house as a ceremonial stage is summed up by Tambiah – 'The spatial layout of the village house is an instructive map of social relations which is incorporated into and expressed in rituals.'

*butsudan – a miniature Buddhist temple in which offerings are made to the family Buddha. Usually located in the best room; sometimes in a room, *butsuma*, reserved just for it and ceremonial usage.

†*kamidana* – *kami* – shelf; altar for making offerings to Shinto *kami* (deities or spirits), located at a high level, usually in the kitchen.

The ceremonial raising of the ridge-pole (*Age-mune -shiki*), carried out on completion of the main structure of the house of Naohi Deguchi, leader of the Ōmoto religious group. The building of an ordinary house too is accompanied by ritual phases

House models

There is frequent use in ritual of house models. In Thailand, a model house is offered to a dead person's soul, if, for some reason, that person could not, at the time of death, go through the usual funeral rites. In various cultures, house models are buried along with the corpse so that his soul might have somewhere to dwell: in China, model houses are set alight and a model of the sacred dairy buildings is used in one of the more elaborate of the Todas's rites in northern India. Among the Ainu of Hokkaido in northern Japan we can find several such examples. Prior to building a house, a small wooden tripod is set up at the spot where the hearth is to be – this is known as the 'house-image' (*kenru*, or *chisei inoka*) and is removed before the purification of the site; another is put there in its place, remaining there until the roof has been thatched. (1)

Another small Ainu house model is called the 'House of Evil', and is employed in exorcising evil spirits from a sick person. There has also been a custom of building a model house to be burned as an act of propitiation to the spirits of the dead. We can find in many cultures, examples of 'dwellings' (house-shaped), for spirits and souls. Thus acquainted with such precedents in the use of architectural models for ceremonial objectives, we should not be surprised to find the Japanese *kamidana* often taking the form of a model Shinto shrine while the internal layout of the *butsudan* represents a transistorised version, as it were, of a Buddhist temple. But the situation is rendered more complex by the fact that the most simple kind of Shinto shrine is called *yashiro*, meaning literally 'miniature of a house', and its prototype is evidently taken from the primitive hut. It is obvious, then, that we are in a complex field of borrowings and transformations of architectural scales and meanings and it is better to tread warily for the moment.

Butsudan

The *butsudan* serves as a focal point for much house-centred ritual. *Kezurikake*, believed to be a physical manifestation of Dosojin, a roadside *kami*, is set up in the *butsudan* in order to protect the household. (2) Osore-san, a sacred mountain in northern Japan, is believed to be the point where the earth makes contact with the next world; located there is Gokuraku-no-Hama (The Shore of Paradise) – white sand is dug up from there and used to fill the incense burner of the *butsudan* at home. (3) *Senzo-eno-wakare* indicates the bride-to-be farewelling her household and ancestors before the *butsudan*, prior to going to the groom's house for the wedding ceremony. She does this after a special morning meal, and takes leave of the various *kami* of the house at the same time. (4) Ordinarily the doors of the *butsudan* are closed, except on these special occasions when they are opened, incense and candles lit, and small offerings of rice presented. In *Nihongi*, an eighth-century chronicle of Japanese history and myth, such a domestic altar is described and thus given archaic credentials. (A.D. 685, Emperor Temmu) 'Orders were sent to all the provinces that in every house a Buddhist temple should be provided and an image of Buddha with Buddhist scriptures placed there. Worship was to be paid and offerings of food made at these temples.' (5) Of late, excavations of pre-historic house sites have revealed small stone altars on which images were placed, thus corroborating *Nihongi*'s evidence. But it must be made clear that not only is the *butsudan* involved directly in domestic ritual, it also governs the location of other ritual structures . . . in Okinawa, it is believed that when a person has been dead for thirty-three years he becomes an *O-kami* (a great spirit or deity); he is made offerings on an additional altar above the *butsudan*. (6)

At *Bon*, the time of year when it is believed the souls of the dead revisit their former homes, there is a special *bon-dana*, or *tama-dama*, erected in the house to welcome the souls of those recently dead and for those of distant ancestors. Also at *Bon*, the

A rather elaborate and expensive
butsudan on display in a shop
specialising in Buddhist articles

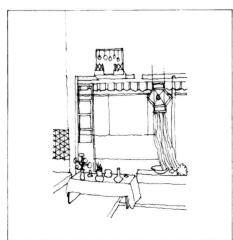

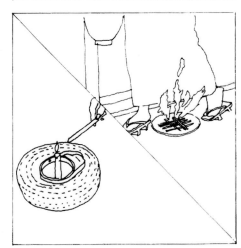

Ritual fixtures in the house at the time of Bon (July 13–15) Right centre and top; *bon-damma*, a modified *butsudan* set up in order to welcome the souls of the dead. Top centre; specially constructed *bon-damma*. Top left; *bon-dana*, made on the morning of July 13. The list of the family's ancestors (*ihai*) is removed from the *butsudan* and put on the *bon-dana* for the length of the festivities. Left centre; *bon-dana* variant, also made of the 13th. Left bottom; in the Kansai area, the *bon-dana* is often set up on the verandah (*engawa*). Bottom centre; a temporary altar (*saidan*) set up before the *butsudan*. Bottom right; a fire is lit at the door in order to welcome the spirits of the dead . . . they are led from the grave to the house by the light of a lantern carried by the household head

A home-made *butsudan* in what had been a cupboard. Aluminium foil was applied to the inside and the various Buddhist effects set up. The photo shows it opened up specially for the village's annual festival (Yabata, Mie Prefecture)

butsudan can be used instead of the specially erected *tama-dama*, with twigs of ground cherry, persimmon and chestnut suspended above it. Hence we can imagine that one of the reasons for a permanent altar, such as the *butsudan*, to be installed would be to save having to build a new altar each time; another advantage would be that ancestors could be communicated with more often than just at *Bon* and *Shōgatsu* (New Year). Yanagita makes the point that the *tama-dana* and *butsudan* are now separate and can both be employed at *Bon* in the same household, but were originally the same thing. He quotes the *haiku* by Kyōrai in support of his case: 'In the interior of the *tama-dana*, my dear parents' faces.'

Yanagita also conjectures that in the past there was a special occasion when it was necessary to set up a new altar other than the ordinary one, and as it came to be decorated more and more beautifully with flowers and lights, people began to have an idea that it was a special altar necessary for *Bon*, something different from the usual altar, and so in some regions they came not to use the permanent altar at *Bon*. At such times they would move the family tablets from inside the *butsudan* and lay them to rest on the new altar for the *Bon* period, leaving the *butsudan* unoccupied. In the district of Iida, Shinshu, the empty altar is called *O-rusai sama* (caretaker), and the household leaves an offering there. Around Sannohe, it is called *kara-dana* (empty altar), and also offerings of rice are made to it. Robert J. Smith has carried out a very systematic survey of this ritual terrain in his *Ancestor Worship in Contemporary Japan*.

Recently, when some families decided that the *senzo-matsuri* (the *Bon* festival) and funeral rites should no longer be carried out according to Buddhism, they suddenly got rid of their *butsudan* and combined it with the *kami dana*, hoping that it was a more authentic form of domestic worship, but instead of this being a restoration of the past, it remained a new plan with an unpredictable future. 'In my parental home, the Matsuoka family, my grand-mother was a Buddhist, so offerings were made according to Buddhism, but at the end of the third year of mourning after her death, all the Buddhist fixtures, the sutra scrolls, and ancestral tablets were thrown into the river, leaving the butsudan just an ordinary shelf.' (7)

Related to the *butsudan* are the *senzo-dama* and *mitama-dama*, altars on which the souls of the ancestors are venerated, and in some areas the *butsudan* is also called *mitama-sama*. In some households, there can be found not only the *butsudan* and *kami dana*, but an altar known as *mitama-sama*, at which ancestors are worshipped. After the house has been cleaned out on the thirteenth day of December, a light is set up on this *mitama-sama*. In some households, there can be found not only the *butsudan* and *kami-* installations at *Shōgatsu* (New Year).

Choosing an outdoor site was the oldest form of religious ceremony, but in certain situations it became increasingly meaningful to have them in the house. Such fixtures as the *kamidana* or *butsudan* arose from the need for a suitably purified place to hold a celebration inside the house with an intention similar to creating a temporary ritual site outdoors. When the grounds of a shrine were used as a temporary site for prayers and petitions, a small wooden platform was built, branches hung at its corners and offerings made. In case the observance took place inside, they would bring in a board and put it on the floor where the ceremony was to be carried out . . . as skill developed in building, they could make a permanent altar in the house. When we remember the small size and impoverished conditions of most primitive dwellings, we can imagine that usually such ancestral festivals were held outdoors. For night watches in winter or for various performances, rites and feasts accompanying a particularly long ceremony, a part of the dwelling was used instead of putting up a temporary shed for protection from the elements; strict abstinence was kept, there were many taboos, and even now in many villages, adult women are not permitted to enter the inner room in which the *kamidana* is set up. The meaning of etiquette regarding the *tokonoma* alcove, in Japanese houses, is best understood when we regard it as the seat of the *kami*. (8)

Kamidana

'The task of making rice offerings to the *butsudan* and *kamidana* falls on the housewife – if her daughter should make an offering, it means she will be the next housewife of that house.' (9) This brings us to the *kamidana* in more detail, another point on which domestic ritual is focused. From the late Heian period onward (c. eleventh century), a male and female doll, imitating *kamibina*, earlier folded paper dolls, were put on the *kamidana* as permanent amulets. (10) From these developed the full pomp and circumstance of today's *hina-matsuri*, the girls festival. Amulets of all kinds are put upon the *kamidana*, and letters or telegrams bearing good news are put up there even today. 'There are some households who, should they receive a baseball bat signed by a well known player, will place it on their *kamidana*.' (11) In the area from Nagano to Iwate

One *kamidana*, priced at 39,000 yen; in the front are three bowls in which rice, salt, *sake* are put; these are flanked by miniature lanterns of the kind that normally line the route to a shrine. Behind is a miniature *torii* (shrine gateway), flanked by ceramic images of a fox (*Inari*), which is the symbol of the shrine from which this particular *kamidana* is bought. Flanking these are miniature bamboos carrying the Imperial regalia (mirror, jewels, sword). At the back, centre, is a type of mirror, usually installed in a shrine

The house from whose hearth fire is taken in procession to light the main structure erected for the Dosojin Festival, Nozawa, January 14, 15. The *kamidana* can be seen in the background, fresh offerings having been set up on it

A simple *kamidana* in a bar, Ueno City

prefectures, Dōsōjin was considered a member of the family. He was represented by wooden images about thirty centimetres high placed on the *kamidana*. Offerings were presented to him just as to family ancestors. (12) Atsutane Hirata, one of the greatest Shinto advocates during the Edo period, maintained that the family should never turn its back on the *kamidana*. (13)

As the conclusion of the *dōsōjin-matsuri* (festival), Nozawa, January 15, and the *kanjō-tsuna-kake*, at Kinshōji, Nara prefecture, January 8, *kamidana* from the respective villages are thrown into a bonfire. Another part of the *nozawa-matsuri* is interesting in this context; on the concluding evening, January 15, a party go to a house known as *himoto*, from which they are to receive purified fire to light the bonfire. They enter, sit around the *irori* (hearth) drinking *sake*, while a flint is brought from out of one of the many *kamidana* installed near the *irori*; a fire is made from it, which is then transferred to a large straw torch, which is next carried in procession to the bonfire. *Nazuke* is the ritual naming of a baby, held usually on the seventh day after birth, when the father is released from *imi* (impurity); the *nazuke* is hung up under the *kamidana* or from the column of the *tokonoma* alcove, the name written on it, and prayers are offered for the child's future. When someone dies, it is customary to cover the *kamidana* with white paper, to protect it from pollution. On the eve of January 6, beneath the *kamidana* or *butsudan* seven lucky vegetables are used for cooking a special rice next morning, the first 'seventh' of the year. Customarily offered on the *kamidana*, are *sakaki* (a Shinto shrub), rice salt, *sake*, a list of the anniversaries of the dead family members, as well as Ebisu images and Inari lanterns to promote trade. In S. Kyushu, it is believed that there are some hungry homeless souls who might steal offerings from their *kamidana* and so offerings are made to them so they do not go hungry – but this offering is made on a lower shelf than the regular offering, and at the edge. When removed from the *kamidana* it is not eaten by the family, as are the other offerings, but is thrown out. (14)

One variation of the *kamidana* includes the *ebisudana*, found at one end of the *kamidana*. An image of Ebisu, one of the seven gods of luck, is put there, preferably made from the wood of an old bridge – since many people have trodden on that wood, Ebisu can derive enhanced potency from that. On the third day of *Shōgatsu* (January 3), which is Ebisu's special day, *shimenawa* (sacred rope) is put around the *ebisudana*. In Nagano prefecture, Ebisu is believed to leave the district on October 20 and return a month later laden with treasures, so *mochi* (pounded rice), *sake*, and even money are offered on the *ebisudana*. (15)

At *Shōgatsu* (New Year) we can see the *kamidana* most dramatically in action. The first day should be opened with propitiating prayers to the gods and the spirits of one's forefathers before the *kamidana*. (16) In Nara prefecture, for example, a special *kamidana* is erected in the *okunoma*, the best room, usually entered only on special occasions such as this. The special *kamidana* is known as *ehodana*, and its function is to welcome *toshigami*, the New Year's deity. (17) In other regions we find that special shelves were made, *tochitokudana* (soil-profiting-shelves). They comprised a plain new board, hanging between two straw-ropes fixed to the ceiling in a prominent place. Offerings were made on this board, which was oriented to the direction from which the New Year deity was to arrive, a direction altering from year to year. During this period, branch

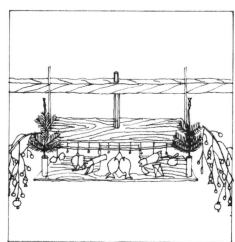

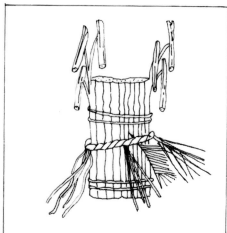

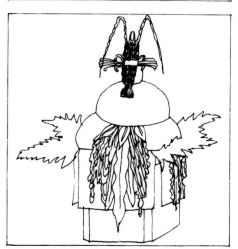

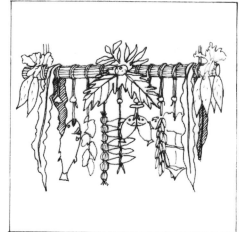

Ritual fixtures in the house set up at New Year (Shōgatsu) Right top; toshi-dana is a separate kamidana for the New Year deity (Shogatsu kami). The structure is permanent but the decorations are renewed. Top centre; this toshi-dana is renewed annually. Top left; kadomatsu – these pine decorations are set up in front of the door of the house to welcome the New Year deity. Left centre; this structure (toshigi or nyugi) is put up in front of the door to ward off evil influences. Left bottom; these are specially prepared beaten-rice cakes (mochi), for the New Year deity, and is set up in the house. After, it is eaten by the family. Bottom centre; in North Japan the altar to welcome the New Year deity can take this form. Bottom right; Saiwaigi, hung above the door (see annual cycle diagram). Right centre; toshi-dana, annually renewed

The variety of *kamidana* in one store en route to the Fushimi Inan Shrine, Kyoto

families visit the main family, the head of each branch family tying *shimenawa* rope onto the main family's *kamidana*. Sometimes a stack of three or five newly made straw sacks of rice are placed below the *kamidana* and considered the resting place of the New Year deity.

Not only are such ritual appliances individually utilised in the privacy of the home, but some do circulate from home to home. One village, in Nara prefecture, has a small Jizo image, in a little house-like case, that circulates through the village, staying in each house either one or three nights. *Gyōja* was the name of a special kind of priest whose function was to visit homes he was invited to and set out in the house the altar he carried on his back – on it were 33 Kannon images, so that the setting up of those images in the house was considered the equivalent of the family having made a pilgrimage to 33 Kannon temples . . . (18)

The ritual enacted in the house opens up for us a corridor that connects with a very primitive core which is the still very much living heart of the house. The ritual moments reveal the full armature of the house; the ritual, as it were, completes the house. Thus it is, at root, acknowledgement of 'houseness'. The ritual in a house opens up for the new Japanese architects a vast field of opportunity which some of them are acting on; perhaps Hiroshi Hara is in the forefront, with his houses creating a kind of ritual topology. We shall examine these in detail in the next chapter.

Life cycle

The house and its *kami* (deities) are very much bound up with the individual's life history: from birth to death, the domicile is the stage upon which the major events take place. At the time of birth the women and children of the village present gifts to the

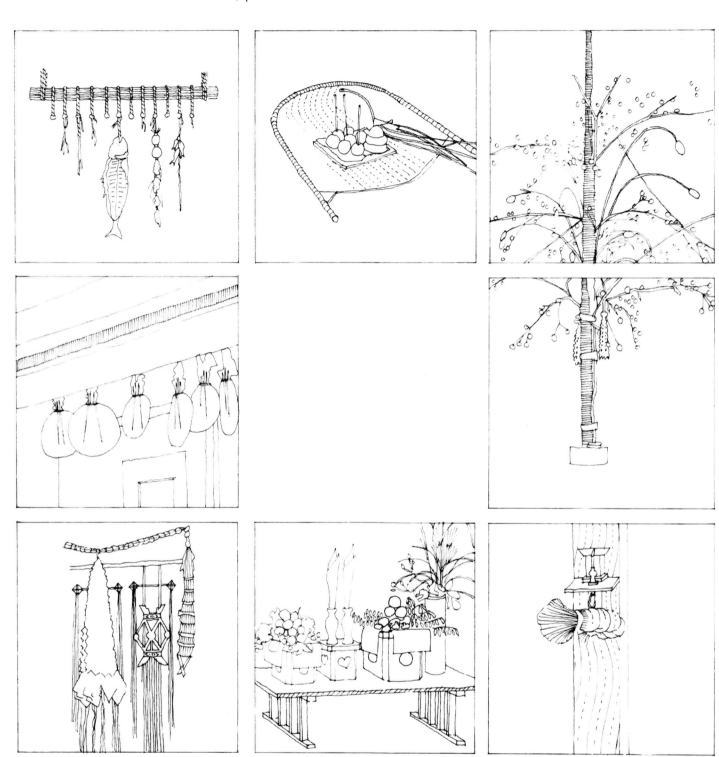

Ritual fixtures in the house, annual cycle
Right centre and top: *mayudamma* – pounded rice in the shape of silk-worms are fixed to branches set up in the house at New Year or 'little New Year' (January 14, 15). Top centre; New Year offerings to the ancestors' souls. Left top; a piece of wood is suspended over the front door, hangers are suspended and fish, radishes, etc, are hung there at New Year. The sketch shows the state it is in on January 20, having been eaten by the family. Left centre; pounded rice cakes are hung from the eaves in winter and eaten during a summer festival. Left bottom; houses are thus decorated at the time of the Tanabata Festival, August 6–8. Bottom centre; these altars are set up on the verandah mid-August when the moon is at its most beautiful. Bottom right; before New Year, the house is purified – the sketch shows the broom used to clean the *kamidana* wrapped with straw and kept in the house after New Year.

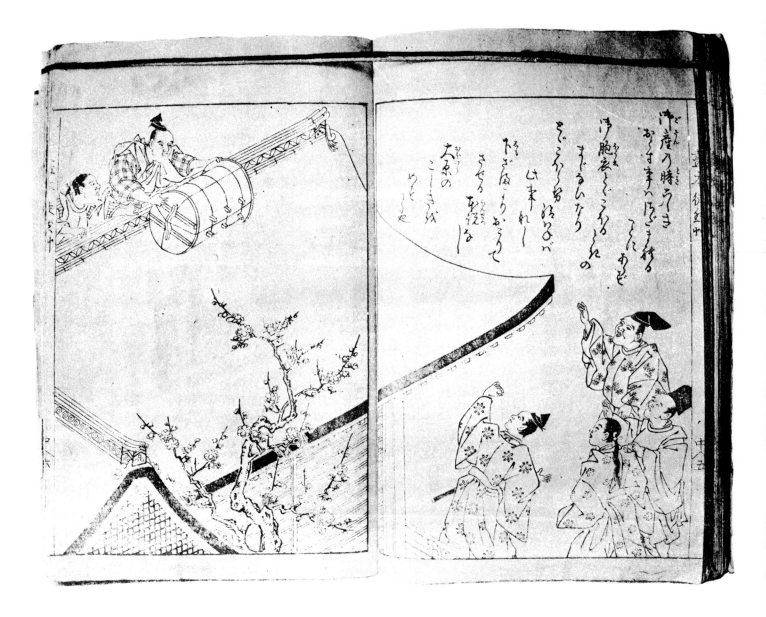

御産の時うま
おぐす（ぐこめも
ぐこの
御胞衣ぐこめも
すぐるひなり
てぐこめものも
ぜこれぬ男
大原の
こしきに
とざばこりおうて
さてろ
さてろ　をのき
ろ

mother and eat heartily of a feast in the house. The child is thought of as being half of this world and half of another – not until it is two years old can it be fully accepted into the family on the occasion of its first visit to the shrine (hatsu-miya-mairi). (19) Nazuke, as mentioned above, is the ritual naming of the baby, yuzome is its first bath, iwai-gyaku takes place a week after the birth when visitors call on the house, offering food (ubu-meshi) to the mother. A fourteenth century document records that women of the Imperial household, in case of a difficult birth, had koshiki rolled from the ridge pole of the palace down to the ground. Koshiki are square boxes with bamboo ends, formerly used for steaming rice, and it is thought that this custom was of peasant origin. (20) Takatori mentions one way to guarantee an easy birth was by keeping the toilet clean, thus the mother-to-be could propitiate the spirits of the house, the deity of the toilet in particular (see below) – should the child be a girl, this propitiation would also ensure that

Dropping koshiki from the roof; this rite was carried out should the afterbirth be stubborn on the occasion of one of the ladies in the Imperial household giving birth. The custom rests on the likeness of sound between koshiki and koshi-ki (pain in the loins); dropping the box indicated getting rid of the pain. The print was prepared for an eighteenth century republication of a fourteenth century classic

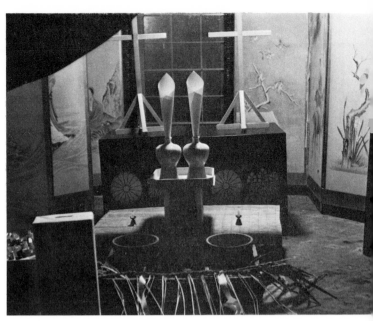

At the times of certain festivals, the houses in the district are opened up – the family heirlooms are put on display and anyone can enter and peruse the exhibition; the night prior to the main procession of Kyoto's Gion Festival is a good case. The two photos

illustrate houses in Kurama, North Kyoto, at the time of its Fire Festival, October 22. The house-as-museum notion is nicely underlined

she would grow up beautiful. (21) In fact, during *desome*, when a baby leaves the house for the first time, one of the duties is making offerings to the toilet deity – this act is called *sechin*. *Taimen* is when guests meet the baby for the first time, *iwaizen* is a celebratory meal, and *hatsu-zekku* is the first boys' day, on the fifth day of the fifth month, that the male child celebrates – carp streamers are hoisted on a pole in front of the house.

The dwelling is also the traditional focus of marriage rites. The future groom visits the woman he is to wed, bringing gifts of *yuino*, which are then set up in her house's *tokonoma* (alcove): this is a betrothal ceremony – after which the girl would begin to blacken her teeth for the wedding proper. Nowadays, instead, the couple exchange rings on that day. (22) *Muko-iri* is another formal proceeding, usually a day before the marriage ceremony itself; *muko-iri* takes place at the house of the bride's parents, and in its full form involves the setting up of trays of offerings in the centre of the room, followed by a lengthy round of drinking consecrated *sake* by the parents and the son-in-law designate, who also hands over gifts to the family. The daughter is not present. (23) The following morning, on the day of the wedding proper, the groom returns to the bride's parents' house and partakes of a morning meal. Then the bride farewells her ancestors (*senzo-eno-wakere*: see above) and in a prescribed manner takes leave of the various house deities. Leaving the house (called *kadode*) in procession to the groom's house, a small fire is lit (*kadobi*: 'fire at the gate') and a rice bowl is broken – this is exactly what I have witnessed takes place when a coffin is carried out of a house. On arrival at

The front of a house can function as a threshold-theatre – here, the procession from the annual Ikuta Matsuri, Kobe, April 16, pauses at the house of one of the shrine's elders, where a dance is performed.

Paper lanterns, ensuring prosperity, are bought at the Fushimi Inari Shrine and hung up in the house. Here we see some in a workshop of a downtown house in Ueno City

the groom's house, there follows a ceremony accommodating the bride into the groom's family – according to Tsurumi she drinks water from their well, or else she must balance on her head the wooden lid of that household's rice pan, while Takatori observes another version that involves the bride walking around the oven three times. (24) The groom's family greet the bride's, the couple drink *sake* in the main ritual sequence (*katame no sakazuki*), women villagers come and help prepare food for the ensuing wedding party. Should the daughter have to share the house with her parents-in-law, she is not considered a full housewife until she has been formally handed a *shamoji* (rice server) by her mother, which takes place by the *irori* (hearth). (25)

The life cycle concludes inevitably with death, and equally inevitably the house and its ceremonial programme is bound up with the last rites. The coffin is installed in the best room in the house (*zashiki*) which is sheathed in white cloth and offerings are set up before the deceased. The coffin does not leave by the ordinary house entrance (*genkan*) but via the verandah (*engawa*) or through a specially made hole in the wall facing the garden, which is then immediately repaired. Those who carry the coffin put on their shoes inside the house, just before taking out the coffin – thus they are allowed to violate the taboo against wearing shoes on *tatami*. Should the coffin exit by means of the verandah (*engawa*), after the funeral it is stipulated no one can leave the house by that same verandah. As soon as the coffin has been removed, the room is swept: sometimes a special gate is made of bamboo or straw through which the coffin passes – the gate is immediately destroyed to prevent the soul from returning to torment the villagers. (26)

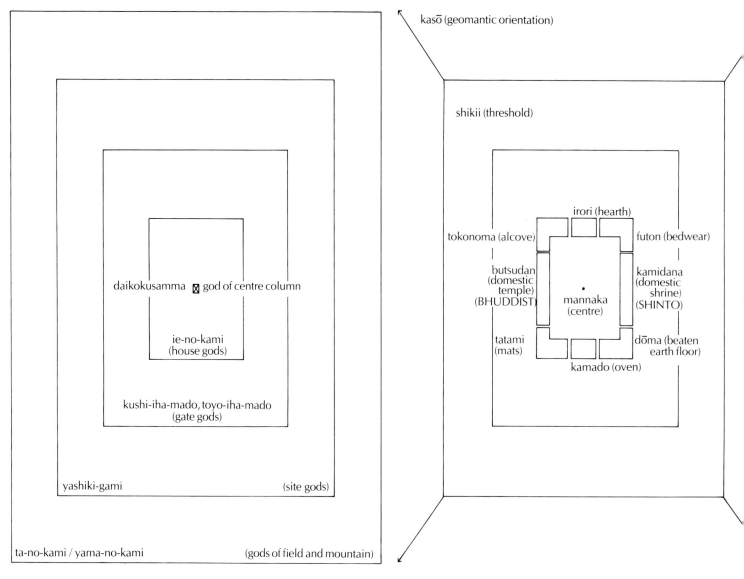

Hierarchy of house deities

Hierarchy of house elements

At the time of a death in a house, or some other grave misfortune, the fire in the oven is renewed. (27) In some districts a kind of *shamaness* (*itako*), within a week of the death, will summon the dead after the funeral ceremony in the home of the deceased or that of a near relative. (28)

House deities

The Japanese have a veritable pantheon of house-gods (*ie-no-kami*) who protect and look over the individual's household. The deity who presides over the site of the house in general is *yashiki-gami*, often enshrined in the garden or just outside the house. Each family may have such a shrine, or it may be located at the house of the main family. At

At the time of the Girls' Festival, March 3, tiered stands displaying the Imperial Court in miniature are set up in the house. This example is set up in a bank in Kyoto – its associated imagery of 'home' is intended to bolster up the bank's image of security

times, Shinto images are brought from popular shrines and these come to represent that particular household's deity of the site (*yashiki-gami*). Two gate-goods, *kushi-iha-mado* ('wondrous rock door') and *toyo-iha-mado* ('rich rock door') are known to us from ancient prayers offered during an imperial festival, and according to Aston, are personifications of the gates to the Palace. (29) There is a kitchen deity or oven spirit (*daidokuro kamisama*): the oven must be compartmentalised into 3, 5 or 7 (magic number) chambers, and typically one would not be used for baking – it would be decorated with *sakaki* (a Shinto sapling) or pine as a form of offering to the deity. It was customary for a member of a household, in the second month of the year, to purchase at Kyoto's Inari Shrine a ceramic image of one of the seven gods of happiness (*Hōtei*), and install it on a small platform close to the kitchen ovens. It augured well if the family succeeded in preserving the images over a seven year period. (30) The domestic broom also has a spirit – the broom must be handled with caution and never stepped over: when a woman was about to give birth she was touched with such a broom. The deity of the best room of the house (*zashiki-kami*) is playful, pulling practical jokes on the household like disturbing the bed at night, but nonetheless is honoured as a beneficial presence in the household. *Sampo-kojin* is a house spirit prevalent in West Japan, and like the *zashiki-kami* can be quite vengeful if angered, but benevolent if propitiated.

The *oshira-sama* (a pair of puppets) are the house gods in the farmhouses of North Tohoku – in Aomori – connected with the legend of the introduction of silk. There are always two 'puppets' covered with many clothes of white cloth (the more clothes the more auspicious) on which stamps from visited temples can be seen. The covering cloth is of gorgeous brocade and around the neck small bells (*suzu*) are laid. (31)

Yabune-kukunochi and *yabune-toyo-uke-hime* are another pair of house gods of archaic origin, whose function was originally to guard the palace buildings from harm of all kinds, and gradually the peasantry adopted them. The *oho-toma-hiko* and *oho-toma-hime* of the Nihongi and the *oho-ya-hiko* of the Kojiki are also house gods; it is generally believed that during the tenth month (on the old calendar), all the deities pay a visit to one of the premier Shinto sanctuaries, Izumo Taisha, except for the household deities who remain to protect the house. There is even a god of the privy – often a lamp was lit in honour of him. (32) Dolls were placed underneath the privy to entertain the

Variation in location of *butsudan* in rural house types; hatched area represents *butsudan*

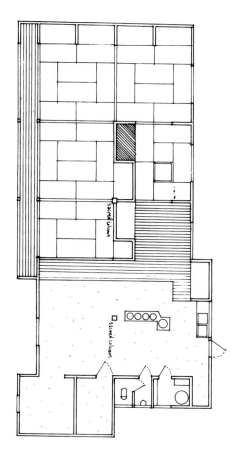

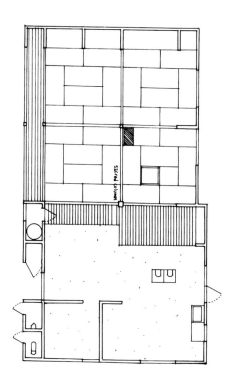

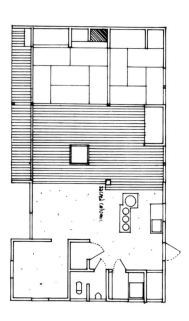

deity; even now, some members of the older generation, on opening the WC door will utter a short prayer aplogising for disturbing the deity. (33)

But exact identification of these house deities is rendered impossible by the way different households recognise different deities – neighbouring families will have quite distinct perspectives on who they are enshrining in their houses, and act according to different ritual promptings. House deities are so much a part of a particular family's mythos that in the end deity and house, family and legend become inextricably one: this could be a working definition of dwelling itself.

Chinese precedent

Much Japanese domestic ritual derives from Chinese precedent – we might consider the equally heavy ritual programme enacted within both the Japanese and Chinese house aimed at establishing contact with ancestral spirits: the house, in both cultures, has been singled out as the best medium for contacting the world of the dead. In the Chinese house ancestral tablets are set up, often in the ancestor's hall. The tablet is generally about twelve inches long and three inches wide, bearing the name and date of birth, and having a receptacle at the back, containing a paper setting forth the names of the more remote family ancestors. Incense is burnt and ceremonial offerings of food are made in honour of the dead.

The Chinese equivalent of the above mentioned Japanese 'Bon', when the spirits of the dead return to the earth, is *Yu Lan P'ê n Hui*; celebrated on the fifteenth day of the seventh month, the solitary souls of those who died away from home and have nobody to perpetuate their memories by acts of veneration are the souls primarily fêted (34).

Ritual in the Western house

But, of course, ritual is not confined to the Chino–Japanese house, or to the long house of the South Seas, the kraal of South Africa or the aboriginal structures of the Arunta. It is alongside us in our Western home cultures . . . the profoundest tissue of house at its most general is ritual at its most genuine. A fruitful start might be made by looking at the kind of ritual appurtenance members of the English branch of the Japanese new religion Soka Gakkai install in their homes. They call it a 'butsudan' (see above) although it bears little resemblance to what Japanese mean by the term. One I saw, which the member had constructed himself from pine, resembled in scale and detailing more a Swiss cuckoo clock, and was fixed to the wall above the sideboard. Enshrined in it was a miniature reproduction of the *daigohonzan*, the original of which is installed in the main Soka Gakkai sanctuary in Japan, on which Nichiren's Lotus Sutra is recorded. Their English language monthly bulletin is illuminating; Barry Martin reports that he had found building his own *butsudan* very theraputic while in hospital recovering from an operation on his cancer of the spine, and he had been allowed to leave after six weeks instead of the sixteen the doctors had expected. Ann Odell contributes another confessional article, stating that when eight and a half months pregnant she had put a

Chinese house ritual; praying before the ancestral tablets

The two Gods of Wealth (Civil and Military), whose shrine was to be found in nearly every Chinese house. Incense was burned before them

card on her 'altar' (she does not use the term *butsudan*) wishing for a painless, safe delivery, which was duly granted her. (35)

The Western house is embroiled in ritual: if it is not the setting up of a cradle or tree at Christmas, it is the burning of a yule-log on the hearth. If it isn't an icon in its iconostasis it is the crucifix in its Catholic corner. If it isn't Sunday roast it's the wine cellar. If it isn't a wake it's a birthday party, an anniversary, a christening, a housewarming, an engagement; if it isn't prayers before going to sleep it's the decoration for a ball. . . . 'He was on the point of conducting him to the drawing room, when suddenly Tchitchikoff announced, with a very important look, that he desired to speak with him on a momentous subject. "In that case, permit me to invite you into my study". (36) The Western house has a ritual anatomy, the room types responding to different phases in the domestic ceremonial: elements of furnishing too . . . "Permit me to request you to place yourself in this armchair" said he. "You will be more comfortable here." "No, allow me to sit upon an ordinary chair." "That cannot be allowed, if you please,' resumed Maniloff with a smile. "My armchair is expressly assigned to guests; whether you like it or not, you must sit in it." ' (37).

'Before sitting down (to eat) she crossed herself in front of the icon depicting the Last Supper, which because of its subject matter had been hung in the dining-room. It was the time of fast before the Feast of the Assumption and there was no meat or milk on the table.' (38).

We need look no further for the kind of sources the ritual affirming architects in Japan have identified and sworn as their own. The works of Hara, Rokkaku, Kijima, Atelier Zō, Ishii, Azuma, Senda, *et al.* have a psycho-anthropological footing in the world of ritual which is both particular and general, pertaining to both Japan and the universe. These architects are not trying to capitalise on the ritual's picturesque formalisation – they are looking to it more unconsciously as the most highly discriminating and distinguished mode of environmental being – the landscape they are trying to practise is not an infantile terrain of ceremonial neuroses but a place that most closely approximates to 'topos' in its richest sense.

The new Japanese house is a 'house-for-an-intersection' of two forces – one a serpentine, dawdling path that connects with archaic and ritualistic notions of dwelling; the other a razor sharp wedge that constitutes the new 'techniques-of-ecstasy'. In this confrontation the new Japanese architect has two alternatives before him – on the one hand, he can affirm the ceremonial nature of domestic life and encourage it through design, while on the other hand he can disaffirm this ritual aspect and all else along with it, ending up with an architecture-of-the-absurd. It is in the light of these polar options that we can best come to some slight understanding of what is going on.

CHAPTER FOUR

RITUAL AFFIRMING HOUSES

Himojii toki ni mazui mono nashi.

. . . I feel that I am responsible for a world I have not created . . .

The sadistic architect aims at making architecture appear abruptly and by compulsion. Man becomes an instrument subject to his every whim . . . the intention of this type of architect is to have man become architecture . . . And at the end, he wants manifest proof of this ensnarement of man – he will aim at making him beg for pardon, apologise, so that he will be forced to humiliate himself, to deny what he holds is most dear . . . 'If the victim refuses to ask for mercy and resists, the game is only that much more pleasing.' This kind of architect has all the time in the world, he is calm, he has no need to hurry. He tests his instruments one by one, employing means to an end that will be automatically reached. This is an architecture of dead possibilities. The ritual-affirming architect takes up an opposite position and goes for an architecture of live possibilities that have a multidimensional being. He is searching out what man and architecture, or more particularly man and house, must be in order to establish the most dazzling correspondence between them. The architect, generally, tends too much to project before himself a certain number of future actions, destined to keep the threats of the world at a distance from him; but for Hiroshi Hara, a representative ritual-affirming architect, that number is without limit – in his architecture-as-perforated-superstructure, space floats from one meaning to another, waiting to take on any job assigned it; that is, it does not reduce the future to its level but accepts it at the level of the future itself. We approach a building – in it we are searching for ourselves; in Hara's projects we come across many such images, hidden about in recesses, beyond cupboard doors, so that we come across them accidentally and they are all the more vivid for that.

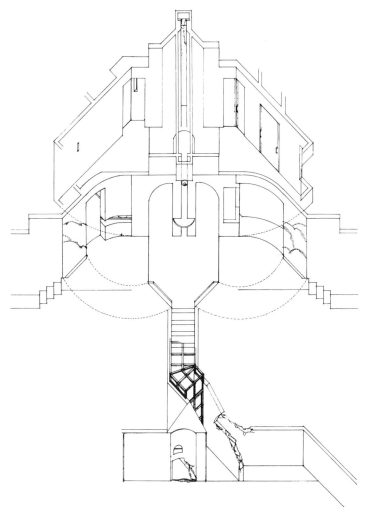

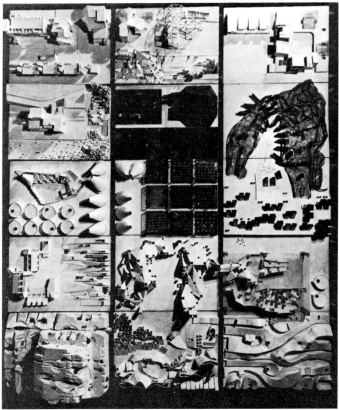

Kumiko Shimada, House of
Interiors
The fixtures and fittings approach

Floating house

Hiroshi Hara, City of Holes
'The basic nature of architecture
is in its holes. The geometric
relations between open and
closed determine what the piece
stands for.'

Every Japanese architect has a theory. Hara's concerns 'floating' and 'holes'. Activities floating *en masse* are the determination of architecture, as opposed to a predetermined, straight line movement. He wants to fabricate a floating space that generates uncertainty, and sees it placed midway between clustered spatial organisations and semi-lattice spatial forms. When he describes Wright's 'flow of interior spaces' as an expression of an axiomatic need to preserve a sense of movement, he could be describing his own work. 'In other words, where one action transfers to another, we must not overlook the interval between the two.' 'I am studying ways to open closed spaces . . . by discovering a variety of opening holes . . .' Thus we can picture his image of architecture as a magic box with clouds floating about the infrastructure pierced with holes. (It's a whole, complete with gaps . . .)

We all want to be the one who establishes reference points and unfolds distances, we all want to determine ourselves over and above others; in the Itoh house, Hara tries to establish a cartographic space in which each member of the household can determine

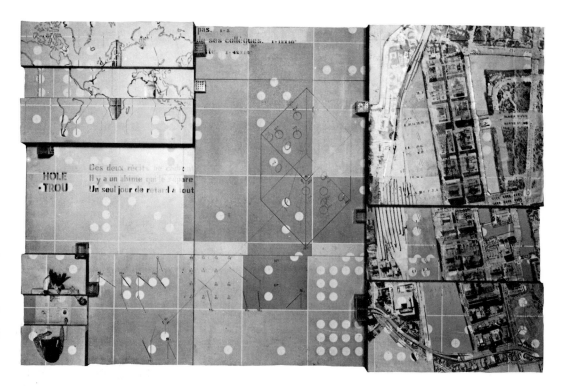

Hiroshi Hara, Hole Trou, 1969
'. . . my theory of holes took the form of closed space at the beginning. A closed space, however, is a dead space. Then, if you make a hole, the situation comes alive. Architecture consists in this transformation of closed space by the addition of holes.'

their own co-ordinates. The origin of this house, with its odd hair-dryer plan, was to create an 'ideal gathering together' . . . the living room 'caresses' those who are in there . . . the sun shines and the stars twinkle through the two 'eyes' in the roof. The Awazu house is more highly calibrated, but the sense of a caressing and gathering together is nonetheless maintained. In the Awazu house, all one has to do is shout out the word architecture to be reminded that it can still have a very foreign and wonderful sound. We cannot push aside its functions and hope to get to the flesh of architecture – in his houses, this one in particular, Hara makes function the flesh and grafts it onto whatever site and client comes along, thus rescinding the critique often levelled at the new Japanese architects that their architecture is purely an invitation to yet more architecture and nothing more. Inside this house we can imagine Hara, the architect, alone and naked, standing before architecture, as though he were modelling for the new Le Modulor. This house is full and dense with meaning. Yet an architecture of indescribable materiality at the same time . . . pure matter throbbing according to a distinctly architectural rhythm, the result being a spatial dance, half Kagura (a sacred dance before the deities), half Tango.

Hara takes a house for a walk, much as Klee did a line, and in his own house we can find this kind of innocence raised to a high level. It is as though he conceived of his life as a dance and planned this house according to the steps of that dance . . . One enters, goes forward and down, forward and down, from side to side, side to side in a long drawn out rite of entry through the extruded space . . . it is patent he conceives of design in an experiential dimension. The house as a whole has a somewhat confessional quality, like a page from a very penetrating diary . . . Following his line back

Hiroshi Hara, Itoh House, 1967
Interior
A pictographic membrane in
which the table, the chairs, the
cabinet, the rug don't appear
incongruous; they, too, are part
of the web

Hiroshi Hara, Awazu House, 1972
Since the space is top-lit, the impression is one of living in the open air – with the sky as roof, natural breezes as air conditioning, it is as natural as a desert isle

Sectional perspective

View of entrance

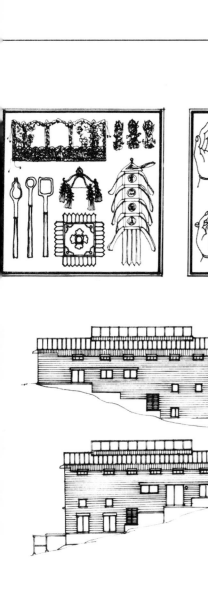

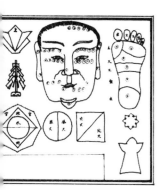

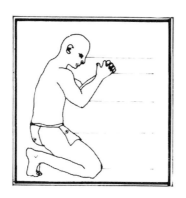

Elevations (71A)

Interior (71B)

Hiroshi Hara, Own House, 1973–4, Machida City

The logistics of a sloping site provide the wherewithal for this Hermeneutic solution. A 'morphological complexity of open and closed domains' that renounces exterior, setting up interior instead, the 'centre' incarnate

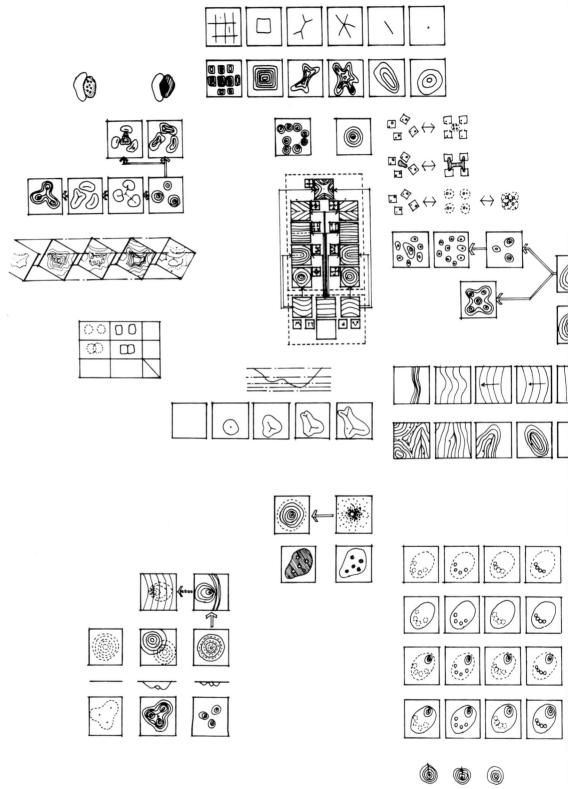

Hiroshi Hara, Thresholds
A collage of his main
conclusions on domain and
village types after the survey trip
to South America

and forth, Hara tests out whether architecture (the house), is a yielding or an advancing. One is reminded, inside, of Inai Norio's collage prints made up from different horizons joined together to form one continuous line.

Always ready to bog down in the materiality of form, basic needs escape by flowing into another form and from it to still another – this is what we see, descending through his house, from the cascades of white perspex to the living space at the bottom of this interior-hill-village. Here we can see form having in a sense taken possession of the house only to have been repulsed; the process recommences, the form reorganising itself and in disguise creeps back up on the house again . . . The space is both retreating and advancing before one in one's comings and goings. On the occasions I went there, like a wasp that sinks into the jam and drowns in it, I sank into that house. I experienced no discomfort, for I had no fear of this dissolution. To touch architecture is to risk becoming architecture . . .

Going down the various levels in Hara's own house, one feels as though one is reliving the sequence of rituals attendant on the building process – first is *jichinsai*, the earth-calming-rite, before construction; the next is *choshisai*, the first use of a saw or an adze; next, *richūsai*, the ceremonies accompanying the erection of a column; the last main one being *jōtōsai* (or *age-mune-shiki*) to celebrate the raising of the ridge-pole. Each drop in level in the house corresponds to another stage in the ritual. Such ritual acts as a safeguard, a series of precautions to ensure that the building in question does not rupture the prevailing environmental superstructure, with its vestigial sacred forces (*kami*), and ensures stability and long life in harmony with a symbolically conceived cosmos. One can sense in Hara's design procedure very similar concerns . . .

House/topos

The ritual affirming architect like Hara sees a building as a theatre of creative occasions, a performance piece that solemnises city as it fêtes it – as he said of his early Induction House (1968) – 'the city is the circumstance of the phenomena occurring within the house.' Hara's houses are exultant, abandoning themselves to a lyrical pursuit of topos: all the devices of threshold are orchestrated in such a way as to centralise the plan. The mid-point is the conclusion of his houses – they begin outside in a flourish of encircling devices that is commemorated internally by a sacred navel, where Eliade's 'really real' finds embodiment. Crossing this threshold into one of his houses is like re-enacting a festive procession – his Villa Kudo (1975) could be seen as a domestic equivalent of the spiral pagoda at Aizu Wakamatsu which enshrines a miniaturised pilgrimage route within one building. Going up to the top of this pagoda and back down again, one passes a number of Kannon figures, each of which represents a temple in the original pilgrimage circuit this reduced version is based on.

The plan of the Villa Kudo, with its bare living quarters surrounded by a covered ambulatory, reminds one of the hierarchy typical of a Buddhist temple – its simple, slatted walls, modest materials and isolated forest location reinforce the hermitage associations. Refuge, sanctuary, asylum, retreat, safe-place, den, lair, lap, hearth, sanctum, cloister; these, and more are suggested in this solitary citadel. The house

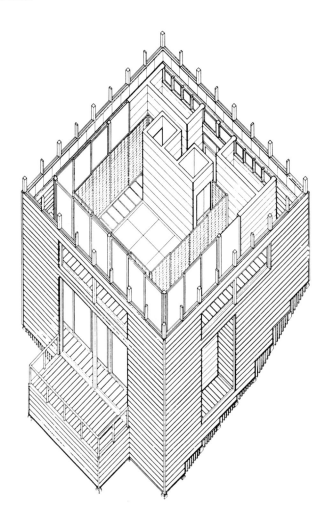

Hiroshi Hara, Villa Kudo, 1975
Axonometric
'World Within Walls'

performs as a life-line with sanity, peace of mind, inner equilibrium. Hara's residential opus is introspective: 'In my house or in the Awazu house I tried to protect the inhabitants against physical and psychological interference from outside. If the house has a strong centre, the pattern of interference is automatically reduced . . . at the moment we are pessimistic and I envision a future in which the last remnant of the natural environment would be a semblance of daylight. The *last threshold*, so to speak . . .' (1)

His houses effectively counter-balance that kind of architecture, neglected and festering, crumbling and ruined, which gives that distinctive taste to a good deal of Japan city. While his houses provide an inexhaustible field for wonder and contemplation, many of the buildings of Japan city have the air of cash registers, collaged onto the existing urban infrastructure. Architecture loses its authority when it goes too far, trespassing upon and trying to disclose things that should never rightly be within its reach. Architecture works best as an irradiation, a diffuse, surreptitious but effective imposition on our senses: it is not theatricalism or ritualised ritual, where architects invent the past, present and future in one ambitious swoop, where nonrealism runs riot, leaving little room for the loaf of bread and bottle of wine: house,

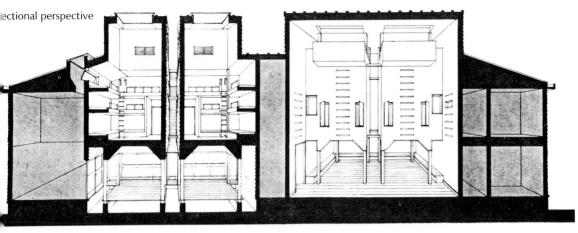

ectional perspective

Hiroshi Hara, Mountain Lodge in
Tanzawa, 1969
Space settles there of its own
accord, nothing is forced,
nothing is presumed, all is given

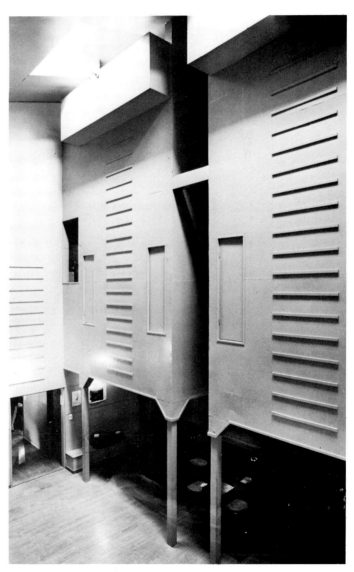

xterior

Interior

domesticity, 'threshold' are shelved while emphasis is placed on pageantry, big texts, a cast of thousands. No expense is spared in the spectacular scenic effects, court entertainments, high flown sentiments; architecture in these circumstances consolidates itself in grotesquely mirrored passions and obsessions. Max Reinhardt's stage sets are brought to mind, as are baroque opera productions, the films of Fritz Lang – but there is no room for 'house'.

Ark house

Hara's Niramu House, 1978, is another rescue operation. It is another ark waiting for the flood. It's another of his buildings closed to the outside world but open to a world of its own designation; 'from the mere existence of separate parts in the direction of a new entity.' In place of 'an overwhelming materialisation of Cartesian space' we find an altar flooded with light from all manner of openings, we find a clearing in a forest, a *caesura*. The hub of the house reminds one of the original Shinto shrines, which were areas of ground surrounded by sacred rope (*shimenawa*) from which offerings were hung. Unfortunately, the house does not enjoy the gently inclined site of the Awazu house or his own, so the space appears more vestigial, less purposeful, but at least it does not become ponderous and the household ritual does not get imprisoned in Hara's virtuosity. His houses proceed 'by a series of little miracles', and we should be grateful for that.

School as house

Hara's schools, which I saw in my first six months in Japan, and remained with me for the rest of my stay, are linear celebrations of the child's environment, the built envelope being exaggerated now this way, now that, as ceremonial acknowledgement of the child's diverse and energetic impulses. These schools are characterised by a constant interpenetration of parts by the whole and their perpetual dissociation and adaptability, the whole sequence rendered comprehensible by a linear processional runway that threads the incidents together; in other words, at the foci of this dynamic flux are points of harbouring and gathering. We can sense, for example, in the Keisho Kindergarten, that Hara envisages architecture as a link in a chain of concrete action . . . In his earlier period, he was preoccupied with working out the riddle behind the organisation of all kinds of things; perhaps through the design of these schools he learned that the riddles must remain unanswered and let go of what had been grandiose aspirations. What was before a greed, an insatiable craving has now matured into something much more honest. These projects illustrate his growing concern to articulate the degree to which architecture is by nature recognition – thus they function as cognitive maps . . . A parallel concern has been to what degree architecture is by nature house.

Alienation is produced if one cannot apprehend oneself in relation to the environment as a cause creating its effects. As one walks through his schools, one has the feeling of discovering for the first time, that not only can one become a cause, but it

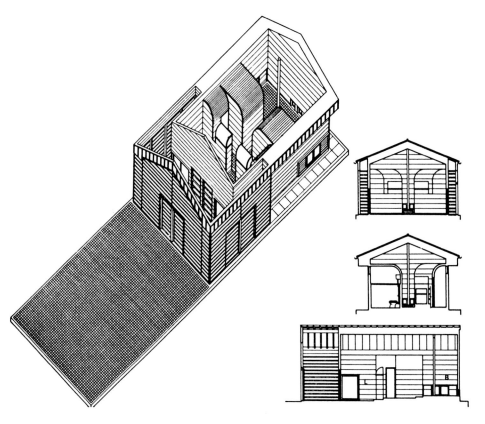

Hiroshi Hara, Niramu House,
1978
Interior
Appropriating the phenomena of
architecture towards the
emancipation of centre from
periphery

Hiroshi Hara, Izu Fishing Lodge,
1972
Sections and axonometric
An excited quiet obtains; the
storm has passed, its excitation
spent

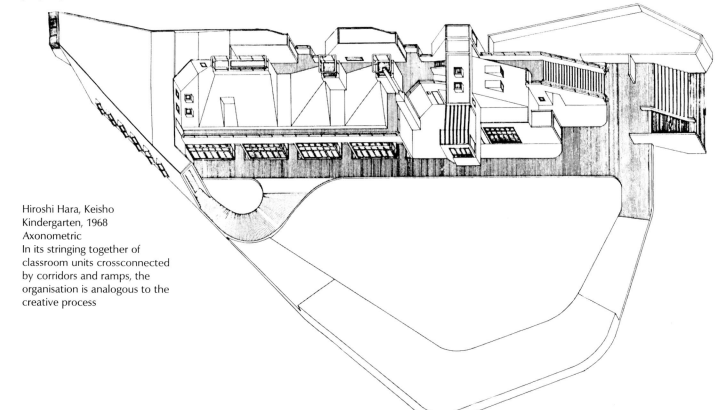

Hiroshi Hara, Keisho
Kindergarten, 1968
Axonometric
In its stringing together of
classroom units crossconnected
by corridors and ramps, the
organisation is analogous to the
creative process

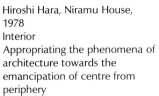

Exterior

Yuzuru Tominaga, Aoyama
House (Inner Void 1), Tokyo,
1973
Like Hara, Tominaga begins
tentatively but latterly engages
with a more ritualising mode.
This early house turns small
planning devices to great
advantage

Interior

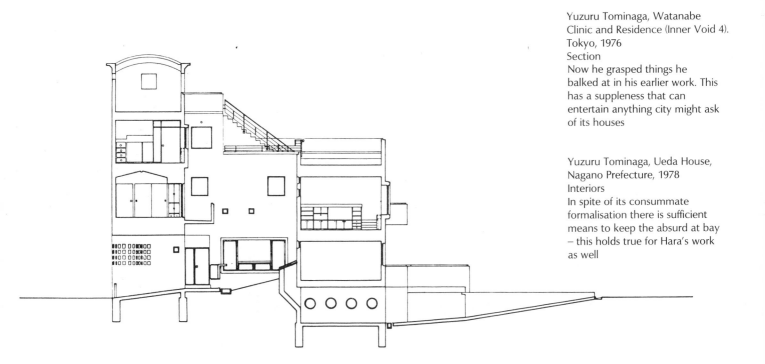

Yuzuru Tominaga, Watanabe
Clinic and Residence (Inner Void 4).
Tokyo, 1976
Section
Now he grasped things he
balked at in his earlier work. This
has a suppleness that can
entertain anything city might ask
of its houses

Yuzuru Tominaga, Ueda House,
Nagano Prefecture, 1978
Interiors
In spite of its consummate
formalisation there is sufficient
means to keep the absurd at bay
– this holds true for Hara's work
as well

Exterior   Interior

Yuzuru Tominaga, Odawara
House, Kanagawa Prefecture,
1979
A stiff architectonic envelope
parodied by its own sinuous
incisions. Here we have two
states of being for the price of
one. It is a not uncommon trait
of modernism (Corb.), but here it
is carried out more irreverently,
like the Gunpowder Plot

is one's right to be one. One is conscious of the field of effects radiating out from oneself: even the inhalation and exhalation of one's breath has surprising repercussions on one's immediate vicinity. One remembers John Cage going into a completely sound-proofed room only to hear the sounds of his own intestinal system in action . . . The schools, abounding in ingenious and playful insights, become a set of suggestions, a precious collection of materials which could be the starting point for an architecture more aware of its own principles. In these buildings, we can find that one idea dominates which then dissolves into another, which by retro-active action is revoked . . . for example, the postulate of sociality might dominate and at other times we are referred to an architecture of encounter, a political will or the tendency of the environment to form . . .

In the schools and playgrounds of Mitsuru Sendah, especially the Nonaka Kindergarten, Fujinomiya city, we can find a similar sensitivity to the world of the child as in Hara's work, accepting their world in its own terms, with its own rites and secret allegiances, rather than assert that it was simply a small scale version of the adult world. This he has done by giving the school a very substantial house feeling, much in the way Hara does, exploiting the house component resident in any building type. This particular kindergarten captures well the real home the child seeks from the environment. The irregular and splintered plan coheres into a dual cosmos, both sheltering and provoking, providing the kids with an elastic environment, at one moment gently succouring, at the next suggesting all kinds of wild games and pranks. The interior, with its miniature stairs and bridges, snorkel outlets, balustrades and skylights suggest a whole and complete world analogous to that of the child . . .

Naming and building

Yasufumi Kijima's fantasies remind us, by their striking collage of occidental and oriental architectural devices, that we must not think of the house as a simple record of certain

Mitsuru Senda and Atelier Man
and Space Nonaka, Kindergarten,
Fujinomiya City, 1972
Exterior
A harbouring, sheltering,
accommodating topos

Akiyoshi Hirayama, K House,
1975
Interior
'This is the fulfilment of the
client's dreams since childhood
of having her own small house
like a dwarf's hut. The geometry
of tangents and my childhood
remembrance of solder melting
helped me to design this house.'
The umbrella-like space created
within is very appropriate for the
creating of an affirmative space.
The umbrella is a kind of
temporary socio-ritual space; for
many cultures, it symbolises
kingship and monkhood. in
China, umbrellas made from
paper money are given as
offerings to the ancestors;
Hirayama's use of it lends the
space a hallowed aspect

Akira Komiyama, M House
(Project 1), Chiba
Exterior
The method the architect
adopted was this; first, eleven
parallel lines were laid on the
site, at ninety centimetres (the
traditional *tatami* module). Then
the lines were lifted very
minimally, creating spaces which
were then, in the final stage,
equipped to support the
functions of house.
Consequently, the project
exudes compactness, with a
distinct nautical flavour . . . the
interior, particularly, calls to
mind a Dragon Boat about to set
sail

data and codes, but as a real involvement in things. He is a dreamer. One of the strengths of the Japanese situation is that not only can the dreamer survive, but thrive. B.O.N. planners are a case in point – they are a group of dreamers, not dissimilar to Kijima, headed by the chief of the cult, Toshiro Tanaka. Their office has no phone – should one want to contact them it must be by telegram. Tanaka says that it's because he does not want to be disturbed, but one feels sure that there is a more mysterious explanation just waiting around the corner. Another aspect of this dream culture is the haunting names that the architects give their houses, such as Yamane's 'Crow Castle', or Itami's 'House with a Wall Torn Open' . . . Kijima's drawings are pertinent; for example, the Villa on a Hillside, Atami, could be a scene from a creation myth, illustrating the birth of the house and its separation from the elemental matter. The drawing of the White House, Minami Azabu, which contains the columns which so shocked the Japanese architectural world by rising from *tatami* and springing up in all kinds of other surprising places, could depict a mythical enactment of the end of architecture and its final reabsorption in the elemental matter. In the more recent drawings of the Good Russet House and the Small Feudal House, the mood becomes more modern, with the house offered up to a psychedelic sky peopled with comets, or else surfing on a Hokusai-like sea. The house designs too have undergone a similar change, from a rather refined tropical baroque to a more concentrated ceremonial high-style.

Affirmation

Could we assert, from the viewpoint of building-anthropology, that it is the act of building that formalises the fluidity of environmental sensations and stabilises it as 'object'? Certainly, looking at the massiveness of the house, Karasujo, by Eiji Yamane (for his mother), one might suspect that its function was to quieten the earth and stabilise things that way ... It is evident that Yamane considers that architecture cannot be contemplated from a distance, but it must invade one suddenly, master one, weigh heavily on one ... The house has a radical spatiality, manifesting an absolute nakedness of built substance, creating in turn a permanent and objective resistance, with all its opacity and impenetrability. The result is a house as a substantial totality, an incorporation of many parts from highly diverse backgrounds, settling together in an upright pose, in the mainstream of *kura* (storehouse) tradition. Such a hand-made, do-it-yourself approach is the affirmation of the basic rights man has over architecture ... Affirmative, but in a different way, is the S. clinic and house by Kazuhiro Ishii. The house is broken down into cubic units, each of which the architect articulates in a distinct manner. The happy-go-lucky screen of windows expresses well the ambivalence of architecture, that coquettish and magical entity, sometimes in the service of man, sometimes eluding him. The fifty-seven varieties of window do a kind of Harlem Shuffle across the front, and one wants to ask the architect – 'Can You Shimmy Like My Sister Kate?' There is the danger

Eiji Yamane, Karasujo (Crow Castle), Yachiyodai, 1974
Exterior
A bittersweet house; the astringency of a persimmon, the sweetness of a lychee

Exterior   Interior

Takamitsu Azuma, Own House, Tokyo, 1967
One of the binary pairs of architectural expressors Azuma employs in his 'Oppositional Harmony' comprises Enclosure and Openness; he states, 'I have constantly insisted that my works become totally cut off from the land surrounding them . . . Creating a rigidly enclosed private realm at first, I devote both prudence and importance to the operation of developing openness.' This house popularised blank concrete and impoverished finishes which were later to be abstracted and used in a more interrogative fashion by Ando, Watanabe, et al.

that the facade of a building indicates a purely external denomination marking the building's external relation to oneself, hiding a blank space with anarchitectural circumference, as is the case with the litho house discussed below, but Ishii's project is ideally divided equally between absolute interiority and absolute exteriority.

The giganticism of the production system

Some architects are more difficult to discuss, for example Azuma and Miyawaki, who, despite innovative starts, such as Azuma's own house-as-urban-salvage and Miyawaki's box-house-running-down-hill-with-a-tree-growing-through-it, have become prone to taking a simpler course. Miyawaki has succumbed to the giganticism that the production system requires of him and designs banks and stores as though enchanted by the

collusion between capital and the fairy-tale that characterises the Japanese economy. But this is true of all Japanese architects, architecture being accepted on the level of merchandise – there is even a glossy monthly magazine called 'Commercial Architecture'. This leads to certain semantic problems. Kazumasa Yamashita, having worked for more than two years in England and Germany, has a high regard for European housing provision, and would like to see G.L.C. type housing in Tokyo. Of course, at the moment, this is impossible; what is possible is that he is invited to design some rather exclusive shops in a fashionable slot of downtown Tokyo, to be crowned by some very expensive apartments. In frustration, he designs the whole complex (From First) as though they were Greater London Council (G.L.C.) public housing, and I am sure that he feels he is being 'social' in doing so. Still, without some such inconsistencies the urban environment could not exist; the urban environment is a gigantic illusion made possible only by the factories and the bureaucracies that are kept out of sight . . .

Takamitsu Azuma, Akatsuka Tower House, 1970
Exterior
Continuity and Separation; 'Inside a single house, demands for spatial continuity and separation exist simultaneously . . . the old system has lost its magic . . . in the past thirty years there has been the development of private rooms for individual family members.'

Takamitsu Azuma, Akatsuka Lodge, Nagano Prefecture, 1969
Exterior
Variability and Permanence; 'In my works, I use concrete boxes with
partial wooden floors, moveable units, high spaces and floor-level
differentials in one-room spaces. I do not use them solely for the sake of
variability . . . but to suggest and accommodate change.'

Takamitsu Azuma, Oyama House, Osaka, 1970
Exterior
Complexity and Simplification; 'In a world in which information is
multifarious in nature and immense in bulk, it is not surprising that
human beings should want their own homes to be simple places where
information is limited.'

Yamashita's Mov Lodge, a second house for a well-known sculptor, possesses a vertical infrastructure much as Hara's projects tend towards a horizontal one. As a result of the skip-floors and the constricted circulation space, one feels that one is forever climbing up inside a Chinese puzzle. He makes inventive use of tiny sites and modest budgets, often coming up with attic-like bowers that Bachelard would have appreciated; particularly the house-with-two-roofs, with its two ocular lenses trained towards the sky. His clean, shingled forms have spawned a whole circle of architects engaged in mutual *magobiki*, (one architect quotes from another architect, who was quoting from another . . .).

The biology of house

'Domo Celakanto' (1972–75), the house for a magician by Atelier Zō – its snaking form as it runs down the gentle incline, its snapping jaws and winking eye are reminders of the anthropomorphic nature of the original house – the Ainu, an ethnic group in north Japan, conceive of their house as a person lying down, his head near the god's window, feet near the entrance, his stomach facing the hearth and his backside hard by the toilet area. In Korea, the ridge of a thatched roof is braided and the word for ridge literally means back-bone. The foundation of a house is known as the foot of the house. Other anthropomorphisms found include the frequent equivalence between humans and columns, the phallic nature of columns, the way the front and back of a house are conceived of like the front and back of the head, etc . . . one only has to remember Dogon cosmology to realise the importance of such tendencies.

(Yamashita's house for a designer in Kyoto with its vivid face in an elevation like a silent scream is too well known to go into here, as is Isozaki's computer print self-portrait in the projecting gallery of his museum in Gumma.) Domo Celakanto rolls down the hill in campaigns of symbolically amorous pulses, metamorphosing into landscape, vegetation, and fish at subsequent level changes. The resultant zoomorphic synthesis is a remaking of nature in its own image, and is therefore strictly 'garden'. But 'house' and 'garden' have always had reciprocal tasks, and here we can see each taking stock of the other, as might have been depicted in a transformation scene of Grunwald. In the Domo Arabeska (1973–74) also by Atelier Zō, the reciprocity is more compromised, and a pantheistic confusion holds sway, while Domo Celakanto is more probative, demonstrative, conclusive – the organic chronometry is sustained throughout, like an exquisitely executed relief map. The ritual it speaks of is unambiguous and redeems the house from what might have been an over-rich scenario.

Yōji Watanabe, not to be confused with Tōyokazu Watanabe (see below), has a corpus of work whose metaphoric allusions are turned to good account – an office building in the shape of a penguin, a high rise apartment complex of prefabricated bus components assembled according to a tree-like plan; more germane to our particular case is an office and house for a pediatrician, completed in 1969, which he has dubbed 'Dragon Fort'. 'Originally, the house was to resemble the bridge of a battle ship, but the plan was later changed to suggest the coiled body of a great dragon.' Its formal prowess is rendered all the more apposite by its calling forth geomantic associations: in China,

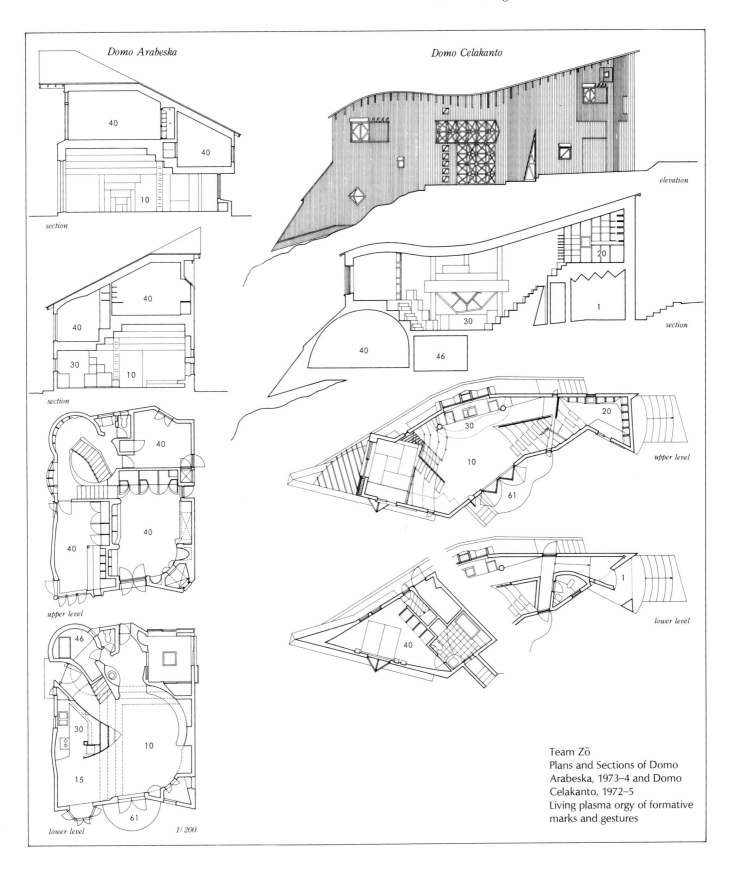

Domo Arabeska

Domo Celakanto

section

section

elevation

section

upper level

upper level

lower level

lower level

Team Zō
Plans and Sections of Domo
Arabeska, 1973–4 and Domo
Celakanto, 1972–5
Living plasma orgy of formative
marks and gestures

1/ 200

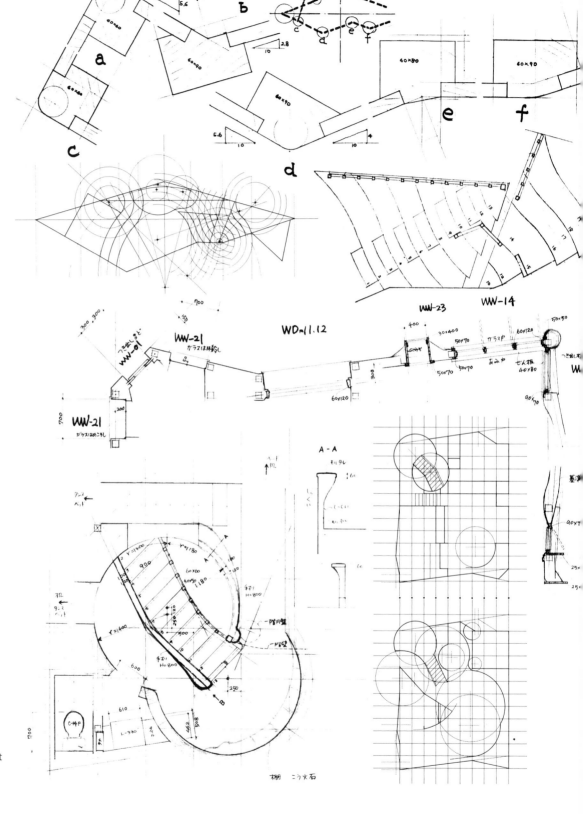

Team Zō, Domo Celakanto
Interior
A house for a well-known
magician; it conjures up and
juggles with all the
unfathomable secrets of house. It
is like a house-warming party
that decided not to end

Yasuo Yoshida, Ota House, 1978,
elevation
Cartoon anthropomorphism

We people the world with a
living architecture.
Top; entrance to Shisendo
garden, Kyoto. Middle; new
house built in storehouse (Kura)
style. Bottom; building protected
from snow by straw matting, and
since it is New Year, the
entrance is flanked by *sakaki*
branches

In the jaws of architecture
Top; decorated doors, storehouse, in a temple precinct. Middle;
decorative curtain at temple gateway. Bottom; Gagaku Stage,
Yasaka Jinja, Osaka, by Maeda

The embodying of nature in culture.
Top; Arata Isozaki, Gumma Museum.
Middle; boutique, Kyoto.
Bottom; Kazumasa Yamashita, Tsuji House

Takefumi Aida, Nirvana House, Kanagawa Prefecture, 1972, front elevation
A chirpy smile on the house's countenance; when primitive man started to build, he couldn't separate phenomena in the way science does; the primitive saw himself as part of a natural continuity that joined everything together, so that when he came to build his own house, in its making he couldn't separate himself from the completed structure – he felt part of the house and similarly saw it as an extension of his own physiognomy. This association of self and house continues unabated in the work of Aida, Yamashita, Yoshida, Team Zō, etc

one of the determinants in locating a house is the 'dragon's veins' that the site may possess – an expert geomancer is brought in to judge. In North Thailand, a dragon is believed to lie beneath the earth's surface, pointing in a direction that changes with the season – it must be propitiated before a house can be built. The spiralling shape of the doctor's house recalls the entrails of deer that were used in traditional Japanese divination. The house squats evocatively on the hillside, commanding views of all around, enjoying a formal and a ceremonial entente with its site.

Architecture might have started by being seen in a vision or a dream – a sleepwalker might have made a sketch of it on sand, awoken and then decided to build it. Nothing is more obscure than this starting point, nothing more crucial, nothing more absurd . . . This is where the occult architecture of Shirai and Shinohara works out, as do these houses by Atelier Zō, Watanabe, *et al*.

Yōji Watanabe, Dragon Fort
(Office and Residence for a
Pediatrician), Ito City, 1969

Rendering of Project; this
biogenetic drama could portray
the secret of life itself; the
structure of DNA comes out of
biology text-books to enjoy itself
before going on to higher things

View from below; just as
the grid organisation of early
Japanese cities was an extension
of the way rice paddies were
subdivided, so this house is a
natural extension of the hill

View from above; an earth-
bound leviathan or a reptile out
of its natural habitat? Watanabe
was a Kamikaze pilot during the
war; perhaps these organic
images are the result of his fear
of losing his own viscera with
each flight into enemy territory?

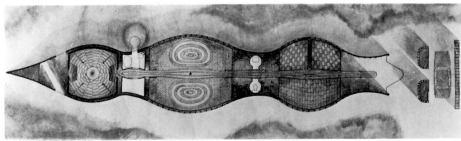

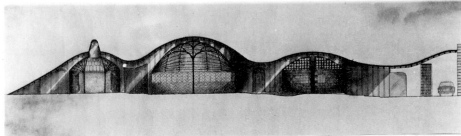

Tomotsune Honda, Long-house, 1979, plan and section
The biology of primitivism

Yōji Watanabe, Yamazaki House, Tokyo, 1970
Street View; in this biology of house, it is the architect's
fungoid touch which distinguishes it from houses by those
arch-Metabolists Tange, Kikutake, *et al.*

Probes into house

The house in Ōmori, by Itami and Takada, with its heavily centralised plan and soaring, monolithic structure has a very powerful, totem-like effect on its immediate surroundings . . . one quickly wants to go along with it, join its side, follow it to the end. Architecture is perfectly understandable inasmuch as one considers it as a history that has elapsed . . . and in this case it is a history that has elapsed not more than a second ago. It is as though its pulse had just stopped and one waits for it to start again, and continue this cycle of death and rebirth, along with its occupants . . . its resemblance to a contemporary-minded church is no accident, I think. It has the precision of a finely perfected ritual instrument . . . As for Hiroshi Misawa, his weekend house 'Shower' is perhaps the most tantalising of his 'Room-With-A-View' series, perched earthquake-teasingly high up on a hillside, overlooking lake and mountain scenery. The form sweeps around its own hub with such momentum one cannot help feeling that it's about to take off. It is a highly tensile timber nest posed above a landscape . . . Dam Dan's self-built tunnels into the unknown are in no need of explanation for the Western architect, since they are the continuation of the 'expo' spirit that he has been familiar with for some while now. This characteristic above-ground corrugated burrow form was first employed by Kenji Kawai, technical adviser to Tange, for his own house, much impressing Dam Dan at the time. Technically, according to Japanese building law, these structures are not buildings, let alone houses, since they

Hiroshi Misawa, Weekend House 'Shower'
Exterior
Pure embodiment of that time-honoured archetype 'house-on-a-hill', Misawa's work calls to mind the shrine set up to the mountain deity (*yama no kami*) prior to felling the first tree for the rebuilding of Ise

Dam Dan, Fantasy House
Exterior
The Wood-Butcher's Art transfigured into corrugated iron

do not have foundations. Irresistibly, the longer versions of these tunnels, such as the stone showroom on the Atsumi Peninsula, bring to mind New Guinea houses of initiation, thought of as dragons . . . The house Poulailler, by Isamu Kujirai, is an example of the raw, impoverished, anti-finish interior quite well favoured for architect's own houses, such as Yoshizaka's or Azuma's; something different from Brutalism, less rationalised, less finished, less closed in. In some of the works of the Shinohara school (see below), we can identify such elements, jutting out like fragments of pure matter, but in the case of the ritual affirmists the brute qualities take on a more esoteric role . . .

Zodiac house versus tragic house

The works of Masahiro Rokkaku are a good note to end this section on ritual affirmists. 'Is House' was built for a radio humorist, well-known for his collection of clocks. His wife

Kujirai Isamu, 'Poulailler', Own House, 1971–
More-or-less complete.
This type of house, self-built, begins in a real sense from the time the first footings are laid – the structure, finishings, fittings serve to confirm the original actions and never bring them to a finite termination – the house probes into the infinity

Doctor's House, Sakae City
Designed by the doctor himself, it has four identical elevations;
The Discreet Charm of the Bourgeoisie

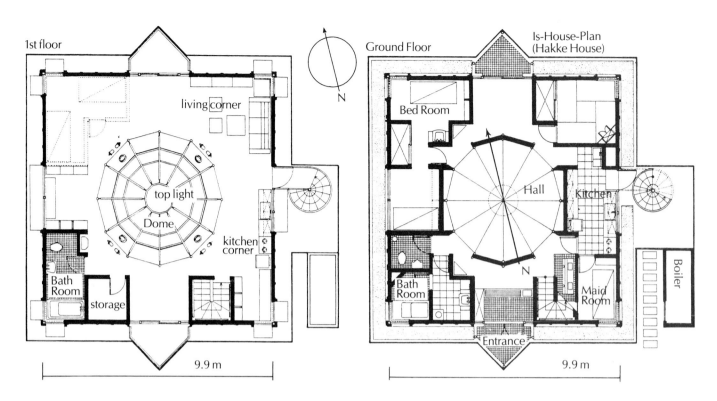

1st floor

living corner

top light

Dome

kitchen corner

Bath Room

storage

9.9 m

N

Ground Floor

Is-House-Plan (Hakke House)

Bed Room

Hall

Kitchen

N

Bath Room

Maid Room

Boiler

Entrance

9.9 m

Kijo Rokkaku, Is House (Ishiguro House)

Plans Interior; the room within the dome
A creative disjunction between sphere (dome) and
cube (overall house), distinguishes this from the more
tragic displacement in Toyokazu Watanabe's
Doctor's House. Rokkaku's is 'Image Processed
Zodiac', Watanabe's is unreal by deliberate contrast

was very anxious about *kasō*, the Japanese form of geomancy; every design he came up with was rejected by the *kasō* expert she was consulting. In the end, he decided to design in strict accordance with *kasō*'s principles of orientation, whereupon the expert confessed he had never seen such a good plan. The result was what he called 'image-processed-zodiac'. *Kasō* is alive and well, even today. A couple in the neighbouring apartment to mine, having had their first child, were eligible for a larger apartment since their apartment was a public one. They were offered a place on a large *danchi* (estate) a few kilometres away. The wife consulted an astrologer, who said the direction they were moving in was inauspicious; she was recommended that they should at least move into an apartment in an auspicious direction for a short while before moving into the other one permanently, so as to mitigate against the worst effects. The wife, however, considered that too much trouble and instead went to a Shinto priest to be purified . . . The family of a friend of mine moved from a town in South Osaka to a location in North Osaka, ignoring the astrologer's warning that the proposed direction was not good. Subsequently the son fell ill, the father lost his job, etc . . .

Despite the eccentric way the concrete dome gets trapped in the domestic space of 'Is House', surprisingly it does not appear to intrude or bring things to a halt. There is not the same intensity or *angst* that makes Tōyokazu Watanabe's house for a doctor in Ibaragi, self-consciously aimed at going beyond Rokkaku's house, a much more extreme

Kijo Rokkaku, Kon House Elevation
Ideographic House. The character 'kon' means money or gold. Aida produced a house-project based on the character 'ie' meaning house . . . this ideographic dimension is nothing new; farmhouses have traditionally carried the name of the household on the ends of the ridge-pole, and the gable has often borne the character 'mizu', meaning water, as a protection against fire

Kijo Rokkaku, Own House, 1979
Interior
'This edifice is a product of my ever-pulsating inner architectural desire to uncover the originality often left undetected and overlooked by many.' His desire was for a house like a telescope, 'Attracted to the eye-piece one sees a wonder-world.'

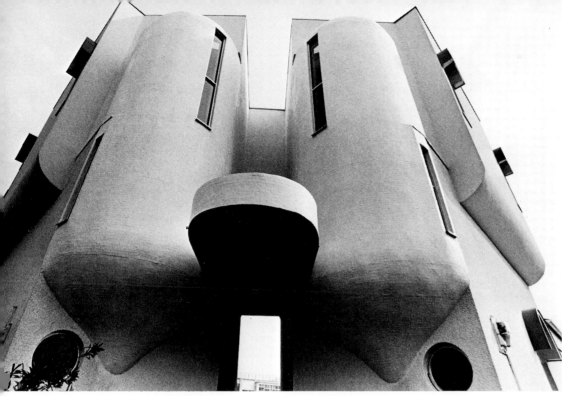

Itsuo Kamiya, Apple House
Exterior
There is something of the
haunted house and Dracula's
Castle in this gothic vision. In its
bifurcation it speaks of the way
everything can be broken down
into its constituent halves

Itsuo Kamiya, House
Garden View
The twin halves of architecture
need not necessarily be taken
vertically, as in the Apple House,
but horizontally as here

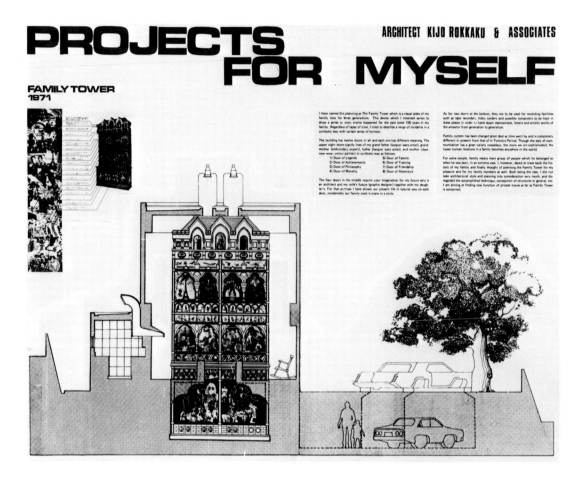

Kijo Rokkaku, Own House,
Project, 1971
Genealogy of house

statement: in the doctor's, the occupants are forced to become passive and pick up what they can from the house, in true architecture-of-the-absurd style. Aware that architecture is a way of hiding the emptiness from himself, Watanabe's programme was to crystallise that, asking such difficult questions as, 'When it is said that a plan is flexible, what does that give us . . . freedom for what?' Rokkaku, conversely, operates on a more explicit level, and the space make-up of 'Is House' is evidence of that – one could imagine people spontaneously being attracted to the dome and starting to walk around it, taking their time, looking it over, just as circumambulation is the core of much ritual . . . Similarly, in the project for his own house, the proposed section, featuring a kind of super-collage of his, his parents' and grandparents' lives, suggest analogies with the Ancestor's Hall found in Chinese houses and the genealogical records decorating the walls of Roman houses . . .

CHAPTER FIVE

A PAUSE

Mishima and Abe: For and Against the Ritual Environment

With no Japanese architectural writers willing to commit themselves one way or the other, it seemed best to conceive of two novelists: Mishima, the first, as spokesman for those architects who affirm the ritual environment, and secondly Abe, spokesman for those against ritual and promoting an architecture-of-the-absurd instead.

As far as Mishima is concerned, the environment is a remarkable fusion of nothingness and vital power, the one wrestling with the other in a miraculous succession of limbs, covered with sweat, now posing this way, now that; should we run through some of the images we have of the houses by Hara, Yamashita, Rokkaku, etc, the overall impression would be what Mishima describes. But for Abe, the nothingness wins out – just look at the work of Suzuki, Ando, Monta, etc, from below, where we can see it weighing down everything, corroding all meaning. For Mishima, ritual is a way of establishing something, even if only for a second, whereas for Abe, ritual can only reproduce the absurdity it is trying to cope with – this is the crucial distinction between Rokkaku's Is house and Watanabe's house for a doctor. Mishima, like Sendah, loses himself in the environment, becomes a captive of it, feeling it bear down on him: only after a Herculean effort can the environment be made tolerable – for Abe, as for Aida, no effort is possible.

For Mishima, whatever misconceptions we might have about things, they can be brought to rights by a single line of poetry, a single rite, or a single house by Kijima. Abe maintains that any act can only undo itself, leaving things just as they were, their inertia undisturbed, as in the U-shaped Itoh house. Though Mishima cannot explain how, things happen, the environment works out, we are able to go about our job, able to build like Yamane's Karasujo, without too much going wrong. According to Abe none of these things can happen – just look at Fujii's projects. For Mishima, the environment is tragic, while for Abe it is absurd . . . The tragic is an elliptical route through the existences and events occurring without relationship to oneself, but whose route forges a link, however artificial. In Abe's eyes ,the absurd is a drip that falls from a tap and splashes onto the sink, swallowing itself . . . Mishima admits that through his grief he is able to share in the existence of others, while Abe's grief can only isolate.

Mishima recalls that the reception room of the house he was born in was 'as big as a suburban church'; this obviously had a big effect on the forming of his vision of the environment as something to be maintained and renewed at all costs, by ritual methods if need be, though we may be bored with them.

From Abe's point of view, the world, as represented by the built landscape, is a bounded infinity, a labyrinth where one never goes wrong, a private map where every block bears the same number . . . even if one loses one's way, one cannot go wrong. He asserts that one can never get lost – what he means is that an environment in which one cannot get lost is one in which one cannot exist.

We might summarise: as far as Mishima is concerned, the environment is reality taking its revenge, whereas for Abe it is nothing nearly so grand . . .

CHAPTER SIX

RITUAL DISAFFIRMING HOUSES:

Part One:
From the Sanctum to the Prison

Issun Saki Wa Yami.

. . . I feel that I am not responsible for a world I have created . . .

'Well then, what about clues? Tell me in detail whatever occurs to you.'
'I can't. There's absolutely nothing at all.'

I had come close to 'homing in' on the business of architecture, the single piece of evidence I could verify with my eyes, touch with my hands. A single lens by which I could substantiate, bring to a point of focus, the numberless hypotheses the environment presented me with. Among the infinite projections which produced something like actuality, architecture alone appeared in relief, it alone appeared whole, substantial, dependable. And yet, when approached too closely, it, also, merged with the environment's countless hypotheses and lost all materiality. I was kept circling around senseless facts, trying to explain the inexplicable . . . One had no idea of the direction governing those walking people, where they came from, where they were going. Architecture, the alignment and relation of buildings in a group, gives those people the sense that their drifting, aimless wandering constitutes a direction. Perhaps it was because of the way the buildings' lines converged at a point.

My own senses, fusing with the city, continued to scatter . . . only with architecture did my chances seem better; there was a way of making a way through the grey formlessness of the city, there was a way of salvaging a little bit of sense. But it was not easy – the lunatic rhythm of the passers-by urged on to unseen goals, the whirlpool of neon, the vortex of regulations, codes, repetitions – these all challenged the last bit of sense left in architecture.

'That is what I wanted right from the start. Why haven't you given me such information until now?'

'But am I qualified to do that?'

Then there is the danger that architecture is becoming more and more of a blank, as if continually erased . . . the colour vanishes, the contours and forms are vanishing and

Shin Takamatsu, Komakine
House, 1976–7
Approachway
The architect; 'We must move
our wearied legs till we see the
gravepost appearing in complete
form.'

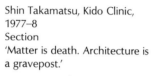

Shin Takamatsu, Kido Clinic,
1977–8
Section
'Matter is death. Architecture is
a gravepost.'

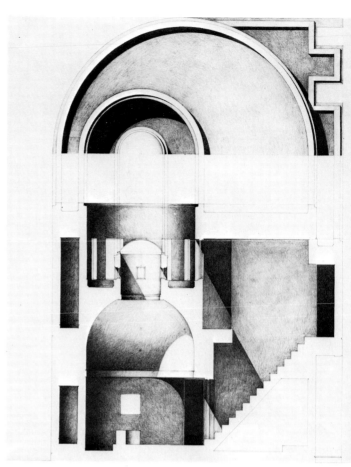

ultimately its very being will be negated, its functions will atrophy; in the city we can witness this now. The city becomes an architect's rendering, with the people rubbed out (or else covered with black crosses).

I was not thrown into a vacuum. Far from a vacuum, it was an immense housing development that stretched away before me as far as the eye could see. The groups of four-storeyed residences, although they were on high ground, had sunk to the bottom of a dark ravine, unfolding an orderly fretwork of light . . . I had not dreamed that such a view would appear. The very fact that I had not posed a question. Spatially there was no doubt the town existed, but temporally it was the same as a vacuum. Although it did exist, how frightening to say that it did not. The four wheels of the car were certainly turning on the ground and there was no doubt that I was experiencing vibrations. Nevertheless, my town had vanished. I should perhaps never have gone beyond the curve. Now it would forever be impossible for me to go beyond it. White perspective of street lights. Crowds of people hurrying home, becoming transparent with every step. I screamed at the driver who had begun to slow down as if to make an inquiry: Turn back, quick! Get out of this development as quickly as possible! I had to get to a place where freedom of space was secure. If it had anything to do with a place like this, I would lose even space, to say nothing of time. I would be plastered into the wall of reality, exactly like the white hand in the restaurant. (1)

Shin Takamatsu, Futamura Office
Building
Axonometric
'The original architecture was in
the memorised form of death.'

Minoru Takeyama, Row House, Hokkaido
Air View
The redeploying of the elements of house towards more abstruse ends; it provides a hieroglyph setting for an abstract society.
Vita activa v. vita contemplativa

Confessions of a student of architecture

Learning is a matter of acknowledging one's own absurdity. The first design one does, whether it be in a school of architecture or an office, one believes in sincerely until it is completed when its absurdity suddenly raises its head. The next design, the one after that and all succeeding ones, follow the same course of belief and subsequent disillusion. Then the architect reaches a stage where he has arbitrarily to stay with a particular decision – he designs, builds and sees it realised and refuses to call it absurd. He relaxes, says he has had enough and continues to act for the rest of his life according to this absurdity held in abeyance. Rare is the architect who will confess the absurdity in his every project . . . and yet, among the younger Japanese architects, we can find some who are willing to acknowledge not only the absurdity of their projects but of everyone else's as well, and it is the purpose of this chapter to first outline generally the absurd nature of architecture and then to examine in detail the way these architects in Japan are consciously creating an 'architecture-of-the-absurd', concretising their attitudes to the absurdity they perceive in the environment.

An 'absurd architecture' is predicated on the fact that there are limits to our human endeavours; man cannot succeed in every scheme he comes up with (some hold he can succeed in nothing) – an absurd architecture thus comes about when intentions are not matched by built form – need points in one direction but the building has gone in another – and the area contained within those radii contains the field denominated by the term 'absurd architecture'.

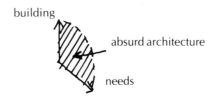

The field of 'absurd architecture'

Our inability to think with our words and our concepts, what happens in the world … Similarly, our inability to build in accordance with need. Our notions are so vague that any act aimed at giving them form, for example, through architecture, is bound to end up absurd. How is the architect to convey through his designs the unthinkable and disorderly succession of present instants …? No ends can be met; once one objective has been reached it dissolves and takes another form, creating the next objective, which in turn dissolves … look at man, look at his desires, his sadism, his homicidal impulses, and his dreams of luxury – any attempt by the architect to make a form, to make a whole from these contradictory postulates is bound to end up absurd. An absurd architecture creates an impossible but fascinating place, replete with enchanting details, witty spaces, charming devices, all calculated to divert us from real needs; such an architecture arises because 'needs', when approached by the architect, have a tendency to slip away … he picks up what he can, labels them 'needs' and treats them as such, designing in accordance with them. This crystallisation of pseudo-need has been the history of architecture … Anxious about the uncertainty of the appearance of needs, in a stochastic sense, the 'absurd' architect tries to outdo them … These are not new themes; what is new is their intensity. In this late-sensate era, there occurs a kind of unavoidable displacement of meaning – whatever the architect tries to do ends up contrary to his plans – he might build for eternity and it quickly falls to ruin, or he accepts the temporary nature of architecture and builds accordingly, only to find that it will last an eternity …

The heart of the absurd

We might well ask the architect, 'Why do you build?' … to which the most normal reply would be, 'Because I am an architect'. Thus we are at the heart of the absurd, if we can say that it has such a thing as a 'heart' … The architect usually does what is necessary to lead him most easily to architecture. It is when the architect feels dead sure of what he is doing, the absurd slips in. The absurd thrives on complacency, self-satisfaction and smugness on the architect's part. The absurd is ever ready to invade should the architect relax, even for a second. The absurd is where we end up whenever the architect takes the easy option … the pleasant architectural wallpaper of the formalists, the walk-down-memory-lane of the eclectics, the geometric order of mass-housing enthusiasts – these constitute an on-going culture of the absurd – the built-apotheosis of absurdity. For in their programmes, man has been relegated to a minor role, as though he had been judged incapable. Thus, an absurd architecture begins the instant the architect gladly turns away from any one of his problems. Such an architect wishes to make our lives smooth and uncomplicated, the environment one of certainty

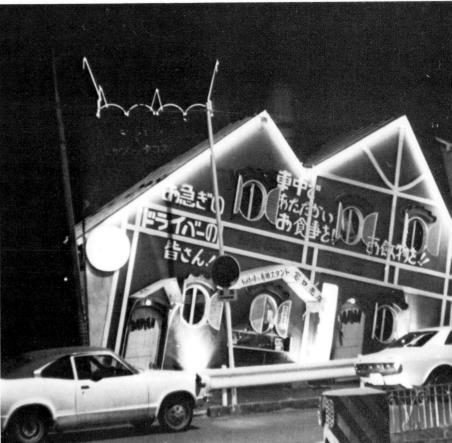

Tatsuhiko Kuramoto, House in Hokkaido
Exterior
Is it sinking? Has it just emerged from out of the earth,
has it just landed, is it the product of volcanic activity or
has it appeared deus ex machina?

Coffee House, Kobe
The leaning house grabs our attention for it is midway
between two archetypes – the new house and the
ruined house. Houses that lean are part of the charm of
ageing and are most associated with rural picturesque

and sureness. Such an architect has forgotten that certainties can only arise from out of
the depths of doubt . . . Such an architect wants unequivocal results and forgets that
they can only be obtained when we have gone through and once more emerged from
the darkness.

The world is composed of collective conventions which impose on the game of
architecture its laws; absurd and gratuitous, these laws have no effect other than to
transform all of man's actions into a kind of environmental ballet. Mystified by these
conventions, imposed on him against his will, the architect is forced seriously to follow
enterprises which end up absurd, which often means without meaning . . . hence we
get to the core of the absurd architecture – it is not wrong, it is without meaning. Or,
whatever meaning it may have is illicit or stolen . . . the clarity that absurd architecture
sometimes possesses turns out on closer inspection to be an absence, the negation of a

semiotic. Even the clearest logic is completely destroyed by the lavish but meaningless form of an absurd architecture . . . the word architecture loses all sense . . . In such buildings, one is plunged without warning into the climate of the absurd, where the everyday and amorphous flux of reality is evacuated; an architecture like a polite nightmare.

The architect is involved in a task whose meaning escapes him . . . he fluctuates between confidence and lack of resolve, between inferiority and superiority complexes. Architecture becomes nothing but a token of these oscillations, absurd, that is, bulging with useless meaning . . . A lack of sequence; architectural events happening apart from time. One detail rarely leads to something else, or follows it. Sequences of events come together and disperse, it hardly matters which. In an environment of chaos, we are lost – in a highly ordered environment, we are equally lost. Unable to control the world, we set up a lesser world – architecture – in order to control that, but in the end even that eludes us. If architecture is said to happen, then an absurd architecture does not happen. An absurd architecture is a scheme of things to keep at bay all that might violate it; an absurd architecture is an attempt to occupy, to claim some territory, to stake out at least the slightest fragment of meaning, or else it is an architecture whose meaning, if there is any, is inaccessible . . .

Absurd buildings annihilate each other's meaning – such an environment eventually breaks down into a kind of fine, translucent mesh, behind which we can see a surging but trapped reality . . . we stand in front of this, waiting for reality to put in an appearance, but we have to wait so long that by the time it arrives, it, too, has become absurd . . .

Disinterested space/encapsulated man

In Tadao Ando's houses, for example, we can see bridges, connectors, links, many intermediary elements, but nothing to lead from and nowhere to lead to . . . the steps appear to be suspended over a void . . . the bridges just hang there, in mid-air . . . To build is to commit oneself, to place oneself on the side of one cause or another. But in the case of an architect-of-the-absurd, he manages to stand outside all commitments one way or another and looks on with an inscrutable grin, aware that commitments get us nowhere. This creates the overwhelming impression in these houses that Ando is designing for steps rather than people, just as in Suzuki's houses (see below) one might be tempted to say he was trying to replace people with light. Ando's houses are always on constricted sites, hemmed in by the daily urban environment; such a location is a perfect setting for a probe into absurdity . . . The symbolic, non-structural column in the Si house is indicative of the kind of language he is learning in order to read and interpret the 'absurd' texts the environment presents him with. The column starts off confidently from the floor, charged with a tremendous phallic capacity, surging upwards, closer and closer to the roof structure, but expiring just below it, as though the effort had cost too much . . . This wilting, unfulfilled column striving to make some sense of a world hurtling unawares on its course to entropy and absurdity, reminds us of the special nature of the column in Japan. One thinks of the heavenly column around which the

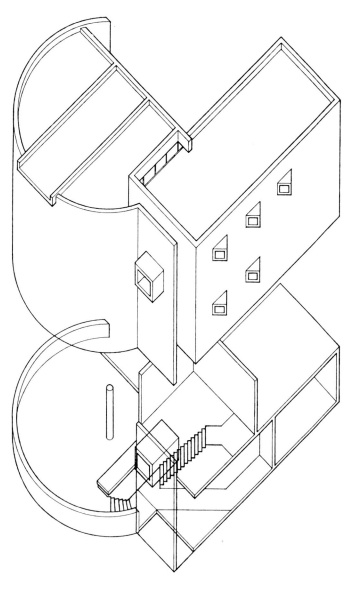

Axonometric

Tadao Ando, Shibata Residence,
Ashiya, 1974

Interior

The orchestration of absence

Axonometric

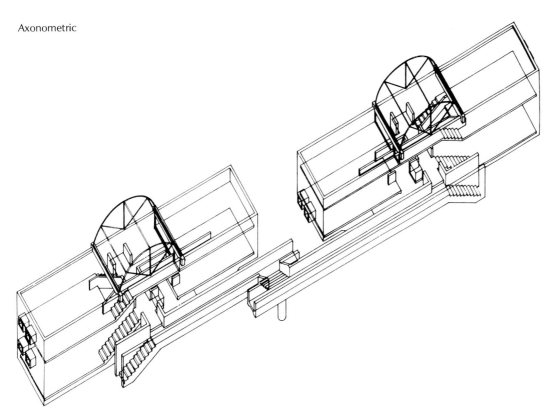

Interior

Exterior

The architect has commented;

'The Soseikan, Y-house, house for two families is located in a typical residential area near Osaka. Setting the two buildings of the same form gives an attractive change to the ordinary outside space. In addition, this distinctive form among non-characteristic buildings around there may also give the impressive expression of the townscape itself.

The Soseikan enjoys the benefits of a site on a small hill in a residential area. Nonetheless, because I persistently wish to pursue the feeling of liveability for the individual, I used enclosure to create a basic space.

In the house I have employed a skylight and a skip-floor (three-level) arrangement, but the inner spaces are unified and unarticulated. The desire to belong and the urge to return to the womb overlaps. I intended to cause the levels – the three-level composition, attic and basement –

to correspond to the levels of human images. The open space with a vault skylight above is the centre of the whole building. Centring on this skylight is the living-room and dining-room on the first floor and on the second floor study and bedroom are set symmetrically. Conscious of the centrifugal symmetry of the building, the south side of the building was enclosed purposely. I created two of these major blocks. They resemble twins connected by an umbilical cord, which in this case is a deck. Though the two blocks are twins, they are placed out of line with each other. The placement suggests a world including the self and other, truth and falseness, on the little hill in the residential district. Over the high spaces are vaulted glass skylights.

At night the sky and stars seen through this skylight suggest that the spaces beneath are an interiorised microcosm.'

Axonometric

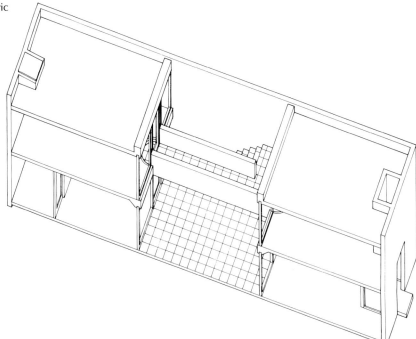

Exterior

Interior

Tadao Ando, Row House at Sumiyoshi, Osaka, 1976
'First of all, an unfinished concrete wall was built on the
property line of the site to gain private space for the
dweller. Its spatial composition is centrifugal, and in the
centre of the house is a light court with exposed
concrete walls, a corridor overhead and heavy staircase.
A front segment of the house has the living-room on
the first floor and master bedroom on the second floor.

A rear one has a dining-kitchen, bath and washroom
and spare-room above. Because of houses on both sides
of the site, openings are impossible, the light court
provides the only contact with the exterior and with the
world of nature, represented by light, air, and rain falling
into the court space and playing an important part in
determining the nature of the spaces opening on it.'

Elevation

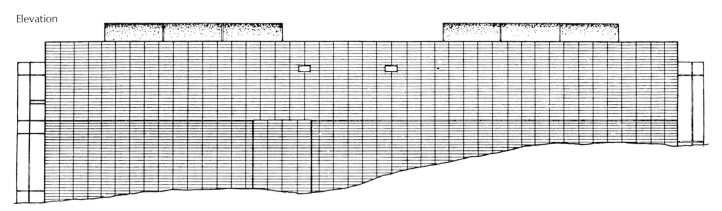

Exterior

Tadao Ando, M Residence, 'Ryoheki House', Ashiya, 1977
'This house is situated on high land, in a National park near Osaka, which is exceptionally abundant in greenery and fresh air. The main feature of this house is a large territory-delineating wall which serves as a façade to intercept the street it faces. This large concrete wall, without openings, completely conceals

Interior

the interior. The artificial rigid frame with the minimum span produces the two blocks with two different levels vis-à-vis the natural slope. The block on the east side has a studio on the ground floor and two children's rooms on the second floor. The western block, connected by a narrow corridor, contains the living-room, dining-room, bathroom and master bedroom.'

Ground Floor Plan

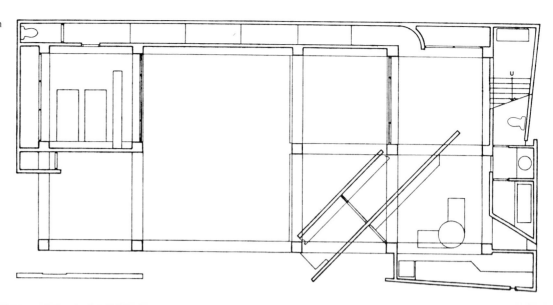

Exterior

Tadao Ando, M Residence, 'Tezukayama House', Osaka, 1977

'Each room is arranged in four grids and two other grids, "void" space becomes the exterior space. The life function related to each room is covered with a wall arranged along the site. A diagonally-arranged wall divides four grids in a terrace, a living-room, a kitchen, and an entrance functionally. At the same time it produces light and shade and articulates time and space. This wall is only a wall containing the meanings. It has been much more effective than I expected and expresses its intention for the town. The beams linking

Interior

the front and rear grids together suggest the succession of equal frames beyond the meaning of a mere frame.

Between walls and frames the light falls and activates the space inquiring the meaning of the frames. The geometric structure filled with intention may produce a common feeling with the emotional city.'

The Glass Block

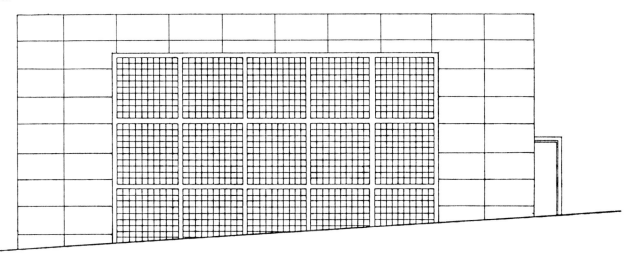

Exterior

Interior

Tadao Ando, H Residence, 'Glass Block House', Osaka, 1979

'This is the house for a couple and their three little children. This house is composed of two blocks separated north and south placing an inner court between them, with a corridor linking these two blocks.

On the basement there is a *tatami*-room for guests and a garage. On the first floor there are public spaces such as the living-room, kitchen and dining-room. And on the second floor there are private spaces such as master bedroom and children's rooms.'

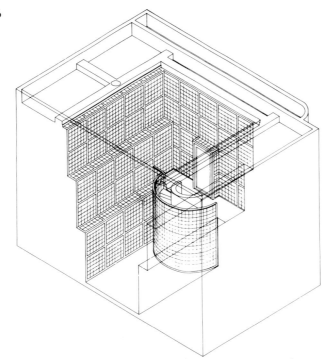

Isometric

Glass-Block details

Tadao Ando, I Residence, 'Glass-Block House', Osaka, 1979

'The building is composed of unfinished concrete wall intercepting the outsides and of a glass-block inner wall which may be thought of as the internalised outside. The plan is U shaped. The building functions are set as the office of the owner's furniture company, and the house of two families, the owner's and his sons'.

Centring the inner court, the northern part of the house is for the parents and the opposite side (southern part) on the first floor is for the office space; second and third floor are for their son and his wife.

With its characteristic of transparency and interception of light, the glass-block wall effects the developing and scattering of light and the securing of privacy.

The inner court is not only the place which provides the connection with nature but forming more structural exterior space and expresses a kind of new world inside the house.

Sectional composition that enlarges horizontally at lower levels makes the gradation of physical volume and closes the inner court.

Light also expands the change of equality of shade and shadow according to the change of floor level.'

celestial pair Izanami and Izanagi circumambulated, generating offspring, in the creation myth Kojiki; the pair going around the column in opposite directions has been interpreted as a primitive marriage rite. The *iwa-ne no-mi-hashira* (the august pillar of the rock base) is the central column of Izumo shrine, a structural part of the building, but bigger than the rest of the columns for symbolic, not construction reasons. As Ise, the *shin-no-mi-hashira* (august taboo pillar) is buried just above the mirror, seat of the sun-goddess Amaterasu. At the Shimo Suwa shrines, Nagano prefecture, each year four *om-bashira* (august pillars) are erected at the four corners of one of its two sanctuaries. The counting word in Japanese for deities is *bashira* (pillars). (2) The way Kijima (see above) deploys his columns is interesting from this point of view.

An architecture dressed up in all kinds of fineries is just as absurd as a naked, raw architecture. A very expensive architecture is just as absurd as a cheap one, a very heavy architecture is just as absurd as a lightweight one, a monumental architecture is just as absurd as a disposable, throwaway one, mass-housing is just as absurd as the single house, planning just as absurd as non-plan, conservation just as absurd as moving-cities. Just how is it that we can fool ourselves by saying that any of these options exactly matches our needs? How can we be for or against, when the polarities put forward are non-starters in the first place? The architect, encircled by so many constraints, is a juggler on top of a pair of cracked stilts on a tightrope over a tank of fire – just the slightest mistake brings absurdity. Ando lights a cigar, sits back and smiles; tomorrow he may tumble, the day after he might not, but he has no control over that, whether he likes it or not. He sits back, relaxes, blowing smoke-rings, living personification of the 'architect-of-the-absurd' who consciously strives to embody what he sees as the most crucial points of the surrounding 'absurd-architecture'. In other words, an architect-of-the-absurd is a running commentary on the more unconscious manifestations of absurdity, as represented by 'absurd architecture'. In Ando's houses, we find that the bottom has fallen out, that in the earth and sky home there is no home at all, that at the root of all belief there is doubt, and at the core of every individual and culture there is absolute nothingness. 'There is no religion that has meditated more deeply on nothingness and emptiness than has Buddhism, and no culture more influenced by such meditation than the Japanese.' (3) Ando's houses act like *haiku*, 'revealing the ultimate emptiness in the minutiae of everyday life'.

The Japanese have gone far to make the no-home comfortable, or to create a no-home . . . and we might find in the houses under discussion here an incorporation of Nishida's view that *mu* (nothingness) might be thought of as a place (*basho*) . . .

Space of departure

There is a consistent mood apparent throughout Makoto Suzuki's houses (real houses-for-superstars; his clients are usually rich, young and famous) – it is as though someone is just leaving, or has in fact just left. Like the houses of Ando, Suzuki's are blank concrete boxes, minimally serviced, with small apertures punched here and there in order to let in light and air. In the photos of the house interiors conventionally shown in Japanese architecture magazines, one could have sworn that the instant before looking at the photo, the particular scene illustrated must have been packed with people; the moment one looks, they vanish, and the atmosphere is definitely one of 'the-party's-over'. One remarkable photo, of the Ta house, actually shows the trailing left leg of somebody on the point of crossing the threshold out of the picture. It could be likened to arriving at a concert hall in time to catch the lingering tones of the very last note of the performance . . . All of this is just to say that though his interior spaces call to mind traps, they are in fact escape-ways.

An absurd architecture reaches out to man, calls out his name, dances for him, sings for him, caters for his every need, pampers him and whispers in his ear; but man does not take any notice, he is oblivious of the attention being lavished on him . . . Whatever the architect resorts to, should absurdity decide to strike, he is lost. Thus, Suzuki, in the Ta house does not go out of his way to pamper man or be in any way obsequious; but on the other hand, he equally does not seriously entertain the thought that his non-action will completely save him from the absurd, it is simply that his position remains rather more noble than were he to try to whisper sweet nothings into man's ear. An absurd architecture is also independent of circumstance – hence Suzuki situates the Ta house without any attempt to identify its location beyond the building's envelope, knowing full well that any such identification could atrophy without a moment's notice. One common place of modernism is the assertion that . . . the world the architect should bring about is a world to be impregnated with always more freedom; Suzuki, sensing, however, that 'freedom' is a frightening thing, does his best to deny it. What he calls 'client-ecology' is in fact a smoke-screen behind which he consciously elaborates his architecture-of-the-absurd.

Whose space?

The U-shaped house in Nakano (1975–76) by Urbot, chief designer Toyō Itō: its strangeness is due to the fact that in order to contemplate it we must place ourselves on the other side of reality, as it were . . . many questions are raised, only to be dropped before they are answered, or else the questions themselves turn into answers, rebounding from the inner wall to the outer one and back again *ad infinitum* . . . in other words, one never gets anywhere, whereas with Dam Dan one does. An absurd architecture arises when the architect tries too hard to solve something that is completely unsolvable, for example, Art Nouveau or Gothic – elaboration beyond elaboration, completely unable to make out in the end. On the other hand, an absurd architecture arises when the architect, sensing the absurdity of that other approach, takes the opposite tack – he simplifies everything to a minimum, hoping to catch up on the problem unawares, but the outcome, ultimately, is as absurd as the former. Architecture, too, always surges forward beyond what the architect had hoped for; or, otherwise, holds back, refusing to meet his expectations. Itō, sensing the twin poles of absurdity that the architect vacillates between, leads this house in a U-shape around the zone of the absurd, demarcating the absurd on one side, the real on the other.

There is something that insinuates itself between need and action; Itō has seized on this insinuation and given it architectural form. Absurd architecture makes out great

Above Left
Toyō Itō, Black Recurrence, 1975
Interior
A long-protracted dissection of house – the chance encounter of a window and a couch on the operating table

Above right
Toyō Itō, House in Kamiwada, 1976
Interior
The stepped elements in the core of the plan could be read as the hour stops on a clock long since abandoned

Left
Toyō Itō, House in Nakano, 1975–6
Interior
Attraction and repulsion unite in this magnetised out-pouring of 'domos'. Circumscribing, intercepting, concentrating . . . an architecturalising of Buddhism's Realm of Nothingness (*Hakoya*)

claims for itself and yet achieves nothing, means without end, form without consequence: its symbolic pretensions are out of proportion to its actual functions, like Seichi Shirai's prick-teasing Noa building. Thus Itō stakes out no claims. An absurd architecture arises whenever the architect designs according to a set of rules, such as Isozaki's 'maniera', Takeyama's 'semiological method', or even Alexander's patterns – the world does not comply with a set of rules, however accomplished they might be – Itō has no time for them. An absurd architecture begins the moment the architect puts forward his intentions, perhaps in the form of a manifesto, as though his buildings could in any way comply with his words – Itō keeps quiet. An architecture placed within limits must be just as absurd as an architecture without limits; just as architecture is as absurd as no-architecture. Solid must be as absurd as void. Those architects with the most profound conviction that architecture has a sense are the most likely to come up with absurd architecture. A simple architecture is as absurd as a complex one, a humanistic architecture as absurd as an inhuman one, a fixed architecture as absurd as an adaptable one – Itō, with this house, tries to be neither one thing nor another, expecting nothing, waiting for someone else to make the next move.

The inessential house

When one passes a building at speed, perhaps in a car, one might take it for a simple and discreet entity and thus find it reassuring and one might be able to believe that there was real blue in the world, real red, real democracy. But, as soon as one holds onto it for a moment, this comfort gives way to a deep uneasiness; it's exactly this uneasiness that Takefumi Aida exploits for his own ends. He wants to expose the myth that we can choose freely, assemble freely and construct the space we want. He mocks the ideal of people confirming with their hands the making of a self-realised house . . . An absurd architecture sets itself up in three dimensions and assigns us roles we are either incapable of or should otherwise refuse. In his most recent house-as-steps, Aida, offers us a very wide range of roles, fully aware that we could live up to none of them – like being offered a fancy wardrobe of clothes, only to find that none of them fits.

In an absurd architecture, the essential passes for the inessential and the inessential passes for the essential. We will find the architect-of-the-absurd, such as Aida, submitting to the two equal and opposite forces (the essential and the inessential), both at the same time. Here, for instance, he is taking the stairs and the heroism that Bachelard associates with them, and the mystic properties of ascension that Eliade endows them with, and by leading the stairs nowhere, as it were, Aida refutes all such oversimplistic formulations, relegating them, with all else, to the trash-can of the absurd, submitting that if the essential nature of stairs can be transmuted thus into the inessential, then this can be done for all the other parts of the house too. The 'absurd' architect exalts the trivial – Mies suppressed the whole world for the sake of a mullion detail. Design in this case assumes the guise of a private rite between the architect and the object of his obsessions; for Aida, in this house, he consciously made the stair the central fetish, and in the previous house-as-a-die it was the window . . .

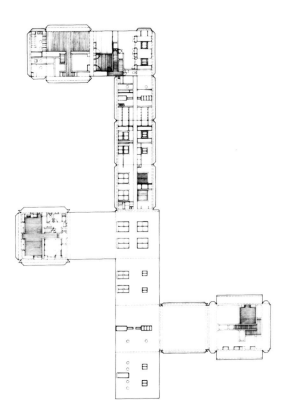

Takefumi Aida
Analytic Drawing, Nirvana
House, 1972

Takefumi Aida, Stepped Platform
House, Kawasaki, 1976
Exterior
Aida has written that . . . 'the
range of view of the architect is
limited – it is as if he were in the
hand of the Buddha from where
he can only see the smallest part
of what is clear to the Buddha's
eye.' He uses 'silence' to
approach the Buddha:
'Architecture can make use of
the silence that exists; take the
case of the expectant humming
of an audience the moment a
curtain opens in a theatre.'

Above left
Takefumi Aida, Nirvana House,
Kanagawa Prefecture, 1972
Rear elevation
'Speculation in the Dark' . . . 'An
architecture of silence is dark
rather than light.'

Above right
Takefumi Aida, Annihilation
House, Kanagawa Prefecture,
1972
Front elevation
'The basic elements of this and
Nirvana House are square plan,
symmetry and white walls. All
these create the sense of things
that one recognizes as having
existed since ancient times. My
intention was to imprison
function within innate forms.'

Right
Takefumi Aida, House like a Die,
Shizuoka Prefecture, 1973
Exterior
'This house was created
according to the system used in
dice and says no more than that
"dice are Dice". House like a Die
has its own limitations, whether
they can be overcome depends
on the architect.'

Suspended house, deferred space

The M. House, by Hayashi and Tomita, is a primary cube whose every face is pierced by a grid of circular portholes: the interior is a complex affair of precast concrete units set on a variety of levels that call to mind a city. In this house we can detect a 'logic of explosive space', maintaining and renewing at each instant the world inside, culminating in a multi-level, cross-connected, highly variegated microcosm of the absurd outer world. On entering this house, one might be assaulted by something like a whirlwind, one finds oneself lifted up in a helical onrush of elemental sensations. All the different parts of one's body vibrate at different speeds, one could be a particle hurled into heavy water for one's atomic spin to be determined. One finds oneself impregnated with architecture: it takes over in a single and dramatic arc. . . The house was used as a set for a television drama, and in the climax it was made out to have exploded . . . its impact, ordinarily, is explosive too. But it's as though the explosive force has been frozen, with the shrapnel caught and fixed, trapped between explosion and implosion; we are reminded of the sense of unfulfilment and absurdity generated by the column-without-a-function in the Ando house, or Aida's stairs with nowhere to go. An absurd architecture comes about when the architect divides his concentration between present conditions and possible future developments – such an architecture gets stranded between the two time zones and languishes as a result. The architects for this house, Hayashi and Tomita, thus deliberately located it mid-way between those two tenses, interested in setting up an architecture-of-the-absurd, like the theatre-of-the-absurd, in which the irreconcilable nature of the different demands time makes on us is rendered with a stark realism. Other related phenomena under interrogation in this house include the fact that architecture is singular, whereas society is plural – to bridge this gap, some architects try to universalise their singularity, but end up by losing even their singularity . . . this is an absurd architecture. Likewise, the architect is subjective but architecture is objective. . . To sum up, the M. house is like this: invited to a banquet, one takes a seat at the head of a table packed with important people; madrigals and other charming ensemble pieces are being performed; servants are in attendance to look after the every need of the guests, but there is one thing missing: the food, for Hayashi and Tomita, the architects, have made off with it . . .

Nowhere, nothing, no way

Despite the interior like a church, reminding us of the house Mishima was born in, what could be the nave in Tōyokazu Watanabe's Nakauchi house (1974–75) is deprived of any real purpose, all there is instead is space hanging around, waiting for an opportunity to be made sense of. As in his earlier doctor's house, with its *tatami* room, resembling an abandoned parturition hut* stranded under a soaring but pointless Renaissance dome, the 'absurd' architect tries to confer anything he may on an environment which flees him. Watanabe accepts the subjective nature of architecture and the architect's role within it, but without presuming too much in his turn. He is symptomatic of many

*Small huts, separated from the house, in which girls experienced their first menstruation, women gave birth and dead bodies were removed there before the funeral – some can still be seen in Japan.

Exterior   Interior

Toyokazu Watanabe, Nakauchi
House, Nara, 1974–5
The architect puts it thus:
'This house stands among the
old and historic houses in
Yamato Koriyama. The façade is
identified with the environment
by making it similar to the
Japanese traditional storehouse,
whereas the inside is designed
like a chapel of the West. In
other words, this house has the
theme of the contradiction
between inside and outside.'
What looks like a gift-wrapped
box of chocolates turns out to
be a time parcel-bomb. The gods
of this house are angry

Toyokazu Watanabe, Kimura
House, Osaka, 1975
Interiors
It has been said that
'This house is romanesque,
whereas Nakauchi house is
gothic. The plan shape of the
void in this house came from
latin cross. It means the absence
of a latin cross – in other words,
the absence of Europe existing in
Japan.'

Exterior

Toyokazu Watanabe, Own House Extension (Gakinoya), 1976, Nara

He has surrounded his old house on two sides by a thin wing of concrete residential space; it could be said that he is putting his old house in a kind of museum setting, the new addition acting as the updated and revised explanatory text. The new interior is a claustrophobic living tunnel bent at right angles.

Watanabe explains;

'Gakinoya (House for the hungry ghost), my own house
This house is two metres wide and twenty metres long.
The inside is like a concrete cave, and is linked to the already built wooden house. There is a contradiction between everyday life and non-everyday life.'

Interior

Toyokazu Watanabe, Nakano House, Hyogo, 1979
Exteriors
From the monolithic lower floors to the upper ziggurat form there is a distinct vertical hierarchy; is the stepped pyramid form there to invite the deities to step down for a drop of *sake*, much as Aztec versions were?

of the new Japanese architects in that he stands at the rim of the crater, looking right into the 'absurd', and rather than try to outdo the absurdity and thereby play into its hands, he makes a small offering to it in the hope he might receive special dispensation to continue his work a little longer. The proposal for capturing his own house, surrounding it with a concrete extension and then replacing his old house with a new unit, is typical of the way these architects are prepared to duck in and out of the 'absurd' environment . . .

Yuzuru Tominaga
Odawara House
These interiors allude to the
existential-minimum of
Shinohara.

Subtracting space

The houses of Kazuo Shinohara have been exerting a strong influence on many students and new architects' projects especially fascinating with the negative possibilities of

house, of creating a house whose meaning lies before it, waiting to be filled in, embodying what Sartre had to say of trees. 'They did not want to exist, only they could not help themselves.' The golden mean, the geometry of the ideal villa, etc – one immediately feels the arbitrariness of these relations – they no longer bite into things; the houses of this 'school' are investigations concerning exactly this thing, the illogical workings of the architecture machine, though they might also be regarded as current reworkings of an old Isozaki theme, *aki* (vacancy).

Shinohara and his followers have contributed a distinct category to the Post-Metabolist debate. A cursory glance at his houses from the outside would just leave one with an impression of nothing more than a slightly dumb, unexceptional formula, and one would be inclined to wonder what all the fuss is about, why is it his name is on every Japanese student's lips and vies only with Seichi Shirai as the architect's architect in Japan

Below left
Kazuo Shinohara, The Uncompleted House, 1970, Interior
'From the viewpoint of designing, his is a process of 'deed' . . . the act of designing involves skeletonising the structure of 'deed'
Below right
Kazuo Shinohara, Tanikawa Residence, 1974. Interior
Towards the . . . 'disintegration of architecture as a whole. "Disintegration" as a phenomenon corresponds to "freedom" as a circumstance.'

Akiyoshi Hirayama, H House,
1979
Model; interior
'This is one way of seeking out
the image of space man had
before he possessed language.
There is another helpful clue for
me, though it is very obscure; it
is "déjà vu".' The interior, with its
Shinohara overtones, comprises
a 'lonely crowd' of characterless
space definers, simulating an
anonymous boulevard, 'Leading
from nowhere to nowhere'.

– Isozaki is, to the practising Japanese architect, an upstart in comparison. One has to pluck up a lot of courage and penetrate deep into the paradoxical folds of his houses before one can discover what it's all about. For example, when we are told that in his House With An Underground Room (Tokyo, 1967) there is a room with a beaten earth floor, we immediately assume that it would be found in the basement – this makes the surprise so much greater when one enters to find the earthen floor comprises the Ground-Floor. His houses accommodate a great many such thrusts and uplifts. It is through the manipulation of such devices that he has achieved the apotheosis of 'house', and it is this quality that has made his work so much discussed in Japan. His programme is uninterrupted homage to, long extended offering to and devout confirmation of 'house': he is in no rush to get to 'housing'. He has, over the years, in concentrating on the single-house, projected himself with such commitment to 'dwelling' that we are obliged to recognise his depth of sensitivity in spite of the modest size of the field of inquiry. His attention to detail is microscopic and his intuition of texture, space and material all point towards 'dwelling' of the most pure kind.

Beginning in a traditional syntax, he was suffocated by the cramped results that such a vernacular necessitated, in the grip of modern economy. The unrealisability of the archaic space of traditional dreams made itself felt, and some new equation was needed; he turned to blank concrete walls, earthen floors and characterless space definers (in others words, ones with no predetermined meaning to them) in order to amplify the delicate schema of the old historical lines. The vignette was a re-enacting, within the house, of what was going on in Japanese culture as a whole. His work turned more towards an existential-minimum, and it became an increasingly internal affair; witness the Cubic Forest House, or the Tanagawa Residence. He took the external characteristics of modern architecture complete with its aloof blanks, and turned them inside out, parodying them with his bleached, featureless, numbed interiors: Mr Shino's house, 1970, with its ambiguous interior void, is a case in point '. . . it may be said that the courtyard as the exterior space has been completely transformed into an interior space.'

Shinohara demonstrates the historical course that has brought architecture to its knees in the contemporary metropolis, and has charted the way it has been perverted into a degraded approximation of need. And this kind of architecture, bound by the laws of supply and demand, inhibited by bureaucratic codes, debilitated by the planners' misconceptions of his role, is no longer an 'environmental trigger', but in fact curtails and terminates the urban flows. We 'make do', 'get by', but only just about. The future lies in one of two directions: we become architecture or it becomes man. Which course is it he recommends? It is basically one of creating '. . . operationally abstract space with a view to producing a new quality of the extraordinary . . .'. He plans '. . . to express the eternal, one of the most radical expectations of man . . .'; in doing so, he has advanced form '. . . substantial symbols to insubstantial, fictitious ones . . .', culminating in 'uninhibited pleas for a characterless, disinterested space . . .'.

After producing some houses that were reminiscent, in a somewhat funereal way, of lost traditions he came up with a house that was a deeply spaced ritual chamber, christened 'Cubic Forest'. His striving for an 'existential-minimum' appropriate for

'dwelling' prompted a good deal of student interest; projects of a decidedly minimal character, sub-tending towards zero, were soon produced – the birth of the 'Shinohara School' was at hand.

Itsuko Hasegawa's Tokumaru house, at Kamoi, with its legs spread wide apart, dividing up living functions into abstract and abstruse categories, achieves a clinical dissection of 'house' and is an instance of Shinohara's influence. The house, any house, is impossible, and she welcomes this impossibility with open arms, taking it against her bosom as though it were 'house' itself. The house at Sayama by Teiji Noguchi, or more especially the house at Nagareyama by Kazunari Sakamoto, share the enthusiasm for the absurd that Shinohara fathered. Sakamoto's work, with its bare windows punched through the flimsy concrete walls without much conviction, with its ladder pointing up, which doesn't seem convinced that up is necessarily the best direction to take, with its space not fully sure that domestic functions are the most appropriate for it; we are in the centre of the doubts upon which the architecture-of-the-absurd is predicated.

'An architecture of negativeness'

. . . looking at something, trying to make out what it is . . . a house as an atmosphere with a scheme for position imprinted on it . . . map-space-allocation . . . vocabulary as recognition of space use . . . architecture as a space graph . . . the association and con-

Above
House in Yaizu

Left
Exterior Stationery shop
in Yaizu

junction of cubes *in vacuo* . . . clocks and clouds . . . one cannot tell whether they are colour or black and white slides, whether they are upside down or not . . . the house as a time-lapse system. (Notes from a slide-show by Hiromi Fujii.) Fujii houses are gridded, sheathed in grey panels or blank concrete, and an anonymous stereometry holds sway. As the architect designs, his convictions fluctuate – at one point he believes firmly in this, next he believes definitely in that, so that often, when actually built, the building ends up as a kind of stream of negative ions sucking away all those contrary beliefs that went into its making. It is the interdependence of this vacuum and the supplementary belief system that Fujii continues to ponder in his residential projects as he tries to discover why a certain kind of architecture, as beautiful and as hard as steel, has the capacity for making people ashamed of their existence. His field of manoeuvres revolves around the various types of 'absurd' architecture:

1. with no meaning
2. with over-optimistic meaning
3. with over-pessimistic meaning
4. filled with useless meaning.

But he goes ahead cautiously, for not the least part of the architect's absurdity is his obsessive attempts to cope with that very absurdity, the architect becoming a comedian in spite of himself. Fujii is careful, in the Suzuki House (1971), the Miyajima House (1974) and the Todoroki House (1975), not to get too involved with this comedy of errors, and treads warily hoping that the absurdity he is examining does not swallow him whole. (4)

Sukiya-tradition or sensory deprivation?

One obvious point of departure for the ritual disaffirming architect-of-the-absurd is the *sukiya* tradition: 'sukiya' is a word derived from the tea ceremony developed in the sixteenth century, and at first meant a secluded place in the house used for tea drinking, but it evolved into a separate tea room within the body of the house and next into a distinct building used exclusively for the tea ceremony, placed in the garden of the house. (5) *Sukiya* then was employed to depict a building that was more or less secluded, more or less enclosed, a microcosm of withdrawal and meditation; a refined, highly artificial place evoking the humility and pathos of a bare hut. The *oeuvre* of Suzuki, Sakamoto, Fujii and other architects of the absurd, with their melancholic, internalised atmosphere, is in great part an inheritance from the space bondage of traditional *sukiya* concepts. (6) But at the same time, the history of *sukiya* has been transmuted, held together, by references to prisons, places of detention, asylums, and reaches a critical point in the architecture-of-the-absurd. A more contemporary and relevant precedent could be the various experiments in sensory deprivation begun in the sixties, in which solitary confinement, the minimising of stimuli and 'brain washing' were examined. It involves the restriction of a man alone in a small cubicle where he can perceive neither light nor sound – the conditions of confinement resemble certain parts of the indoctrination procedures practised by the Chinese communists in the Korean war. The experiments at McGill University confined adult males, one at a time, to a small lighted

Plans

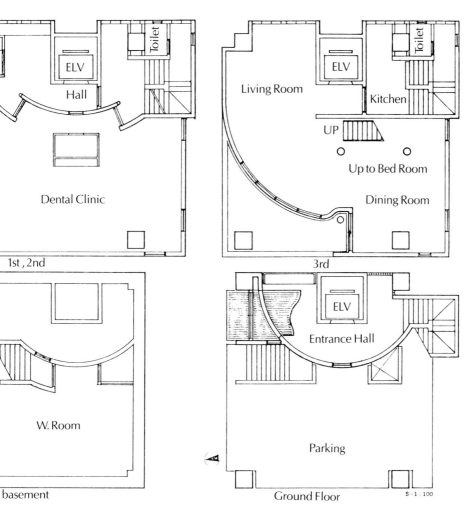

Information

ELV

Toilet

Hall

Dental Clinic

1st , 2nd

Living Room

ELV

Toilet

Kitchen

UP

Up to Bed Room

Dining Room

3rd

W. Room

basement

ELV

Entrance Hall

Parking

Ground Floor

S=1:100

Yasuo Yoshida, Nishiyama House
The architect comments;
'Born in the town without
seasons
Grew up on the hill with no wind
I go out of the house without
any dreams
(Shigeru Izumiya, "Spring
summer autumn winter")
This poem is neither a satire on
the age nor a critique of our
situation. It claims to us lost
visions, insisting the importance
of questioning ourselves what
today is and where we are. We
can see from the dark and
oppressive images in the poem
that we are living in the age
when the meaning of life is
exhausted and yet we can't find
the exit from there. We can also
see in it the desolate image of
modern architecture. I can find
neither an entrance nor an exit
in it even if I put myself in its
lively period. When one
abandons the way to design by
reason only, one can find a field
where various phenomena are
mingled together, What we need
now is sense backed by reason.'

Interior

Yasuo Yoshida, Taki House, 1974

'The ground floor is a workshop, while the first and second storeys are a house, approached by two staircases and dark, narrow and rough finished corridors.' An unconditional architecture, declaring unilateral independence, writes its own charter as it goes along – situational, it refuses to be tied to any a-priori system and would rather default than follow a code it couldn't respect. This house doesn't 'belong' in an ordinary sense, neither does it live ordinarily – it lives its occupants, it possesses them, it has its way

Exterior   Interior

Exterior   Interior

semi-soundproof cubicle. Each subject was asked to stay as long as possible, which usually turned out to be two or three days. The subject wore a semi-translucent goggle that admitted diffuse light but prevented patterned vision. At Princeton, there were more drastic reductions in sensory stimulation – the subject entered a lightproof and soundproof room, within which was a bed in a cubicle four feet wide, nine feet long, eight feet high. The subject was asked to remain on the bed except when obtaining food or using the toilet. It was located within a soundproof room specially constructed in the basement of Princeton's Eno Hall, using a specially devised double structure. The experimenters listened in by means of a concealed microphone. There was no illumination within the room, and like the McGill version, the subject was invited to remain as long as he could, which normally involved confinement from twenty-four to ninety-six hours. (7)

Suggestibility increased in the subject, he began to count the minutes as they passed, and if he was interrupted in any of his tasks his irritability was very high. But some of the subjects found the conditions soothing, their anxieties were assuaged, and their 'freewheeling' mental state a joy. In other words we might hypothesise that the houses that compose the architecture-of-the-absurd are not a simple case of ritual disaffirming and dissolution – there must always be room for the invention of a new ritual to accompany a new circumstance, which we shall come to again in the concluding chapter.

Yasuo Yoshida, Ota House, 1978
In this house he is trying to express the 'mingled phenomena' of space making by the use of a single material, concrete. Circumscribing the dwelling area is a belt of orbiting architectural elements, delimiting the world within, which has the character of what Shinohara termed 'psycho-pathological space'. Add the 'non-existence of space and time' to 'nature in abstraction', add that to 'fissure space and uncertainty', add that in turn to the 'naked machine'; the sum total is what Shinohara has termed 'savagery' . . . exposed roof structure he has coined 'jungle'; the house heralds a primitivity dormant within us all

CHAPTER SEVEN

RITUAL DISAFFIRMING HOUSES:

Part Two:
From the Cosmic to the Satanic

Monta Mozuna's Anti-dwelling box, executed in 1971–72 in the town of Kushiro, Hokkaido, is perhaps the crucial manifestation of the architecture-of-the-absurd, and he defined it as . . . 'only object, without living function . . .' imprisoned within its box-within-a-box morphology, the client (his mother) exists in a theatre of cruelty; each part of the life functions of the anti-dwelling is an island, autonomous, and in a state of incommunicado. I have gone into it at length elsewhere (1), and will dwell rather on Mozuna's subsequent houses, for they exhibit an extreme reaction to this seminal work.

Three projects followed – the Shibata house (1973), the Okawa house (1974) and the Kimura house (1975), and despite sharing with the former Anti-dwelling certain preoccupations with twins, doubles, analogies, mirrors, and worlds-within-worlds, they nonetheless indicate a projected reassessment of man by Mozuna. The series of three projects he gave the working title of *uchū-an* meaning literally 'universe-hermitage'. He accompanied them with ten manifestos –

Universe-hermitage is a cosmological architecture. Universe, human body and architecture constitute its trinity. Universe-hermitage is a miniature of the visional world; its symbol is 'universal ovum'; it is constructed by following 'ritual rules for the construction of an architectural mandala'. The universe-hermitage aims to follow the example of the demiurgic creation, and incorporates a spatial mythos of mirrored images, maps of legendary cities that can be regarded as four-dimensional. The scriptures of the universe-hermitage comprise rare books full of mysteries, inspirational books, handed down from ancient times, and all the literature of Esoteric Buddhism, Yuitsu Shinto, etc. (2)

Left
Monta Mozuna, Anti-Dwelling Box (Hanjuki), Hokkaido, 1971–2 View of Location: a subversive cube set amongst the surburban debris

Below left
General Interior View; the occupant is given marginal space to inhabit, between the box within a box geometry. The centre is one of containment, whereas in Hara's the centre is a release

Below right
General Interior View; lighthouse associations are strangely evoked – yet, should the lamp be set alight it would surely be to misguide local shipping

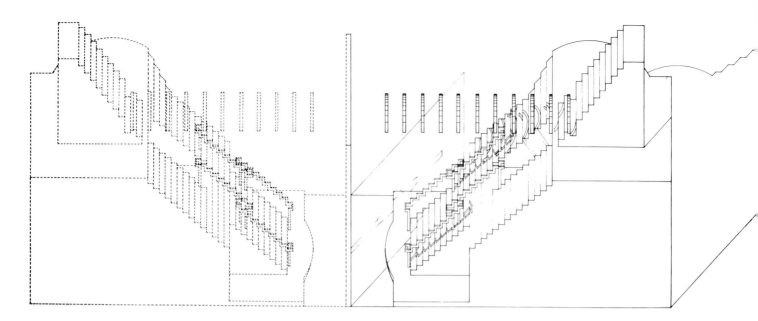

Monta Mozuna, Yosue House, 1979, skeletal notation in double axonometric
For this domicile Mozuna has coined the term 'mirror house'; it might well portray a house deity profaning himself by falling in love with his own reflection

Pondering the trinity

Clearly he was revoking his earlier position on the forefront of the architecture-of-the-absurd, and his next four projects further reformulated his stance. The Taniguchi house, in Wakayama, 1976, based on a layout of stars, he called The Celestial Aspect (*ten-mon*); a project of the same year for a meeting hall on Mount Koya, based on a feminine fertility symbol, was christened The Terrestrial Aspect (*chi-mon*), while the Terada house completed in Kyoto at the same time, came to be known as The Human Aspect (*jin-mon*). The Sumikawa house (1977–78) is a harmony of Yin and Yang.

It is best for him to put forward his present position himself:

> The architectural cosmos has the following three aspects: a Celestial aspect, a Terrestrial aspect and a Human aspect. It is a trinitarian world derived from the universe that is symbolised by Zero. It is also a cosmological architecture that, as a model of the universe, represents the planeto–terrestrial globe. The architectural cosmos contains, as its spatial mythos, a reflected image of the beginning of the world . . . Its sacred structural principle is based on the ins and outs of the mechanism of the universe. The architectural cosmos, in addition, contains another context. The context consists of constructional theories, architectural idioms and structural techniques of modern architecture, and the idioms and techniques of historical architecture. In other words, we can regard it as modern architecture, that which combines modern techniques with archaic symbolism.

The newly completed house in Wakayama, with its column configuration based on a layout of stars, he explains thus . . .

'The Celestial aspect is the "cast shadow" of a celestial figure – the Great Bear – which is projected on the earth's surface. The constellation projected on the earth has seven columns. The Celestial aspect was planned to eliminate the cartesian co-ordinates. It has, like a constellation, various imaginary lines (solid lines, broken lines, dotted lines, chain lines etc), that constitute implicitly a covering structure. It contains Yin-volumes and Yang-volumes.' (We must not forget Kijima's cosmological drawings, and Aida's house-as-a-die with earths instead of windows . . .)

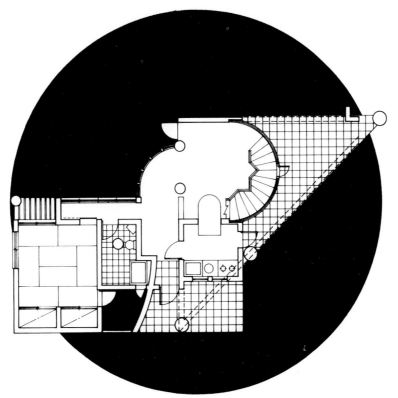

Monta Mozuna, Taniguchi
House, Wakayama, 1976
Plan   Exterior

The Celestial Aspect (*ten-mon*)

Monta Mozuna, Meeting Hall,
Mount Koya
Plan
The Terrestrial Aspect (*chi-mon*)

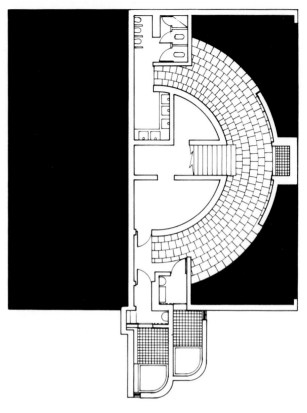

Exterio

Monta Mozuna, Terada House,
Kyoto, 1977
The Human Aspect (*jin-mon*)

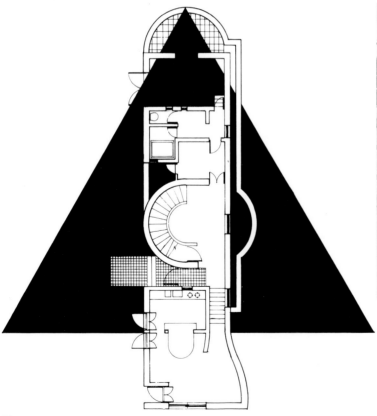

Plan

Cosmic architecture: modernism's dark side

Before we go on to appraise his houses in terms of whether they conform to the category 'ritual disaffirming' or whether this has in fact moved over to the 'ritually-affirmist' camp, as his manifestos would have us believe, or whether indeed they are creating an altogether new taxonomy, it will help if we pause to ponder the kind of area of operations sketched out by a 'cosmic architecture'.

There are a good many affinities between Paolo Soleri's Arcology and Mozuna's cosmic-architecture. In conversation with Soleri, I was anxious to clarify something that had preyed on my mind for a while – sensing something otherworldly in the materio-mysticism of Arcosanti, sensing something cosmogenic in its creation on a virgin spot in a desolate terrain, sensing a city whose continuous hierarchy offered direct contact between the act of having a meal and the most symbolic moment, sensing something faintly religious (in the good sense of that word, not in a derogatory sense tied to a monotheistic absolutism) in the apse-like spaces, the general air of frugality and the emblematic overall plan which appears to engage with the landscape at both the local level of terrain, desert, mesa and the metalevel of cosmic orientations and alignment; sensing this side of the arcological debate, but not being very much helped by his printed statements, I had interrogated several people who had worked over at Arcosanti for short spells, but they all agreed that there was no spiritual quest, and that it was an architectural experience alone.

But managing to pinhole the man himself (not his legend), Soleri was disarmingly frank in admitting the otherworldly aspect – he summed it up by asserting that the most otherworldly ambition he was attempting resided in the imminent properties of matter – that the masterly bringing together of forms is the best recipe for the suggestion of the other side. Imagine a single column lovingly re-embodied, lovingly constructed, squared-up, plumb, a pure manifestation of matter: yet this could perhaps also be the most potent spirituality and otherness that architecture could be charged with . . . Revelation of God, logos, nirvana, truth followed on naturally from the magnificent play of forms in light.

Hand in hand with the development of modernism has gone this extra-real tendency . . . 'Bruno Taut's utopias . . . were an illustration of the cosmic nature of architecture and its religious basis.' (3) The buildings of Rudolf Steiner are very much bound up with his anthroposophy; the work of De Stijl was influenced by Van Doesburg's interest in theosophy; the Bauhaus went through ritual phases. Olgivanna, widow of Frank Lloyd Wright, was an adept of the Russian mystic Gurdjieff, and has incorporated aspects of his teaching into the life of the Taliesin community. (4) Corbusier's design for the Mundaneum, 1929, could well qualify as cosmic for its pretentiously democratic programme: he prepared it for a site near Geneva. The client, a Belgian, Paul Otlet, had devoted his life and wealth to this 'internationalist' project. (5) Ledoux's work, with its guise of rationality but substance of masonic symbols, is symptomatic of the long history of the still to be resolved controversy. The 1960s saw a repopularisation of it – self-build was a reunion with one's original self, the geometrics of Critchlow and Hecker promised a second date with one's original space, and so on. These issues have recently

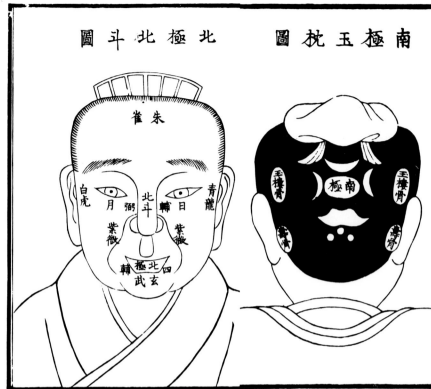

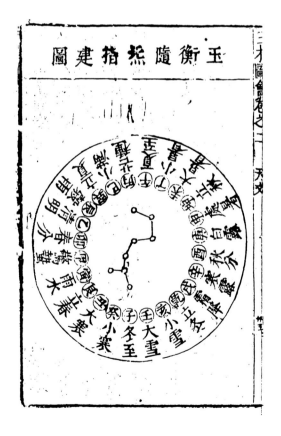

Above
Monta Mozuna supports his designs with these
supplementary images

Left
Diagram of Heaven, Earth and Mankind (with moon and
sun in his hands)
Comparing the front of the face with Heaven and the
back of the face with Earth

A Constellation

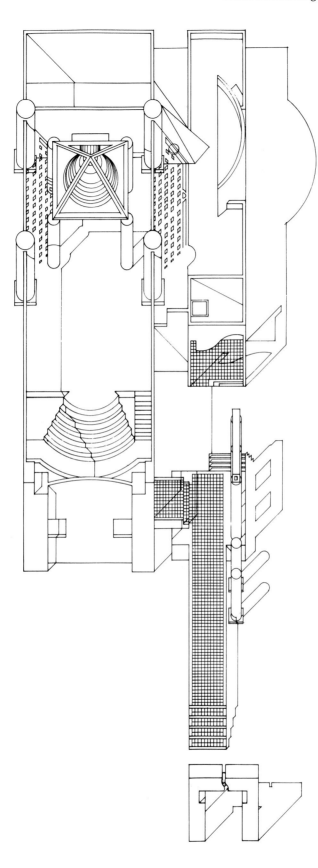

Monta Mozuna, Zen Temple (Eishoji), 1979
Isometric; Second Stage
Mozuna reports that;
'This temple is miniaturised to 1/100 scale of the
passage plan of the famous zen temple in Kyoto,
Myoshinji. The plan recomposed the two systems of
the process of experiencing architecture. The one is
the sign-symbol system of the zen tradition (though
it's common in Egypt or Greece), and the other is the
system of organising scenery (architecture + nature)
which is called "Jukkyo" (ten limits) in zen. In other
words, the order of the former is like this, *Sohmon*
(the first gate) – *Sandoh* (the approach) – *Sanmon*
(the third gate or the gate of the mountain) – *Kairoh*
(the corridor) – *Kyo no niwa* (the garden of void) –
Kidan (the base) – *Shumidan* – *Honzon* (the main
idol), and the latter is the system of the scenes like
columns, the transits, the pyramids of ying and yang,
the inside and outside of the sliced dome, the magic
square, the gigantised *Shumidan*, and the double
mirror images of the Buddha statue.'

been obscured by the flowering of Rationalism, and it is to Mozuna's credit that he should re-open the debate.

But

Yet one feels it is this very reaching forward for a cosmology that negates that very cosmology in the end . . . building according to a cosmology is legitimate in the case of the primitive, who has no choice – for him, it is a natural, unselfconscious expression of the order apparent in his environment. For Mozuna, it is just another ruse on his part to demonstrate that whatever the architect might resort to, he has no guarantee that what he is working on will turn into architecture; however long he might work at it, there is always the risk that it will end up without meaning, plonk in the middle of the 'absurd'. Although this self-styled 'cosmic man' realises that buildings are some of the points of reference man has traced on the earth's surface, in the case of the Celestial house in Wakayama, he wipes all such traces clean, just as a biologist wipes the specimen off the glass plate under the microscope. This house turns into a cosmological vaudeville of the absurd in which the actors gradually decay on stage, so that all one is left with is a group of skeletons dressed up in funny costumes.

Soleri described using the urban items of Arcosanti to frame various ceremonial appreciations of the phases of the moon, sun, the progress of the seasons, anniversaries of the founding etc . . . But we must question the validity of resurrecting these archaisms – all we have to do, for example, is to trace the history of any of the 60 000 annual festivals in Japan to discover that each has a history; its changes in time reflecting differences in socio–politico and economic changes within the community – a change from a system of village headship to an externally appointed administrative post, etc . . . In other words, ritual, if it is to be a natural projection of a real world of authentic space and time, must emerge out of its most everyday roots. Merely to resurrect in simplistic terms certain forms of sun worship would be to mistake metaphor for reality and would impel the arcological city into a tyranny of ceremony.

As for Mozuna's residential designs, one would like to think of them as ritual affirming, only their over-assertion of the cosmological leads one to suspect that he is commenting on the absurdity of any architectural approach, which he more or less admits thus . . .

> I Monta Mozuna, the megalomaniac architect, following the examples of Vitruvius and Alberti, have compared architecture to the cosmos and developed an 'architectural cosmos' . . . As the built 'cosmos' was created by man, its endurance is very short and its scale is very small. Its firmament can be touched easily by hand and its ground can be vibrated or sometimes broken through by a foot. When it is overtaken by a storm, its firmament leaks and its ground is flooded. At a time like this, the 'god' who takes charge of the cosmos must mend in a hurry the leaks in that firmament.

CHAPTER EIGHT

BUT FINALLY,

Is there a ritual affirming architecture? Is there a ritual disaffirming architecture?

The laborious process of causation which sooner or later will bring about every possible effect, including (consequently) those which one had believed to be most nearly impossible, naturally slow at times, is rendered slower still by our impatience (which is seeking to accelerate but only obstructs it) and by our very existence, and comes to fruition only when we have ceased to desire it – have ceased, possibly, to live. (1)

It is all well and good to make these distinctions, 'ritual-affirming-architecture' and 'architecture-of-the-absurd', 'Metabolism' and 'Post-Metabolism', but what do they really achieve? Pigeon-holing helps us to rank and territorialise our experience, based on 'differences', but at the same time this self-same pigeon-holing blinds us to the 'similarities' that bind these designs as much as the differences divide them. Let us consider four schemes, all of which have been built, sharing the common denominator of a cubic grid: Hiromi Fujii's Miyajima Residence, Monta Mozuna's Anti-Dwelling, Isozaki's Gumma Museum, and the clinic by Kazuhiro Ishii. Encountering these buildings in the flesh, it becomes quite clear that Mozuna's and Fujii's with their recalcitrant geometries and context-free grammars, are examples of an architecture-of-the-absurd, while Ishii's is ritual-affirming, owing to its logico-positivity; at Isozaki's one has the feeling that the building had been rescued from Metabolism, of which he had been an early adherent, and offered equally to an architecture-of-the-absurd and the ritually-affirming architecture. The real buildings, then, are inconsistent, individual, and are defined in terms of differences that tend to vanish when they are drawn up; elevations, axonometrics and perspectives duly bring out similiarities, and serve to remind us that categorisation is only a very small step towards an understanding of architecture, which at its greatest depth must remain unnameable, and unknown.

Another qualification that must be appended to the preceding chapters hinges on the very real possibility that an architecture-of-the-absurd might well provoke an updated ritual, more akin to the demands of contemporary society. This is the other side of the Mozuna case – just as his overbearing cosmicity could be the most oppressive, so an architecture-of-the-absurd might see the inauguration of something

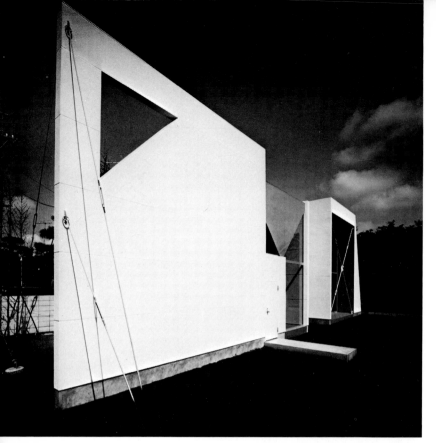

Exterior   Interior

Kiyoshi Nakagome, M and H House, 1978. The evidence presented to the observer approaching this house would lead him at first to judge it esoteric, tangential, denying. But in its inner-directedness there is a sphere of pleasure and enjoyment – there is the neat way timber marries with timber, there is the gregarious and sociable grouping of columns, there is a scale that seems to whisper 'ethnos'

Kiyoshi Nakagome, Architect's Own House, 1977
As in Isozaki's Yano House, here we have a vessel equally charged with the 'Dynamics of Rejection' and the 'Mechanics of Tolerance'. Nakagome's House is both the 'place of arrival' and the 'place of departure'. From the entrance hall up the stairs to the apsoidal study/living space and up again by ladder to the sleeping area is a narrative of escape, like a good thriller

Exterior   Interior

Exterior   Interior

Yasuo Yoshida, Yashiro House,
1977
A house as a city; in this house
Metabolism and Post-
Metabolism are reconciled, an
architecture-of-the-absurd is
resynthesized with a ritual
affirming type. In spite of
Yoshida's addiction to form and
the incontinence of some of its
detailing, it nonetheless totalises
– that is what makes this house
a city. Yoshida not only moves
in on his own volition he turns it
to symbolic account by showing
us exactly how we might follow
it up. Though it might appear
that the atomised particles of
this house were simple, a
'shopping list' of attributes of
house, as yet undigested, what
makes sense of the disparate
items is an energy loop
equivalent to a stream of
consciousness

more momentously beneficial in the long term; in this way, the houses of Mozuna and
Hara, Suzuki and Kijima, Ando and Rokkaku, live in a fundamental equivalence.

Houses: absurd and ritual

Within the work of a single architect, too, we shall find traces of both an architecture-of-
the-absurd and a ritual-affirming sensibility. In this concluding chapter, houses
which exemplify this simultaneity will be examined. Arata Isozaki's Nakeyama
House, Oita (1964), a cubic bastion raised on pilotis, is typical – it runs in the direction of
an architecture-of-the-absurd owing to the external scale being too directly borrowed
from larger projects in his office at that time, while it makes a ritually-affirming move in
its introverted spaces of domesticity. Two Ledoux-like villas by Isozaki, the Yano House,
Tokyo (1972–75), and the more recently completed H. Residence (1977), realised out of a
series of similar residential projects can be similarly understood; ritual-affirming
overtones are evident in the basilica plan and apse-like spaces, while in the negative
interiors, an architecture-of-the-absurd is deliberately conjured up. At the same time,

Arata Isozaki, Nakeyama House, Oita, 1964
View from street
Absurd in its grandiose aspirations, ritualising in its sacrosanct interior

these meticulously trim interiors remind one of the rites of purification that is one of the most obsessive Japanese traits. These enclosed chambers set one to wondering if the seat of a deity (*kami*) isn't enshrined there, and one cannot be sure whether one should not clap one's hands and respectfully communicate with the deity, excusing him for our intrusion. Some of Isozaki's other buildings too, the museum at Gumma in particular, could well be consecrated to some higher purpose, and one imagines they will be rebuilt every twenty years like the Ise Shrines. The vacancy, the absence in his house interiors could also be likened to the barrenness and stark quality of the mountain (Osore-san) in North Japan (see above), where it is believed that the earth meets hell. Shamanesses conduct ceremonies to communicate with the dead – all that is missing from Isozaki's work are the bubbling 'pools of blood' found en route to the mountain top. The houses of Yuzuru Tominaga, Yasuo Yoshida, Toyokazu Watanabe and Kiyoshi Nakagome are similar in their entertaining, without bias, both the ritual and the absurd.

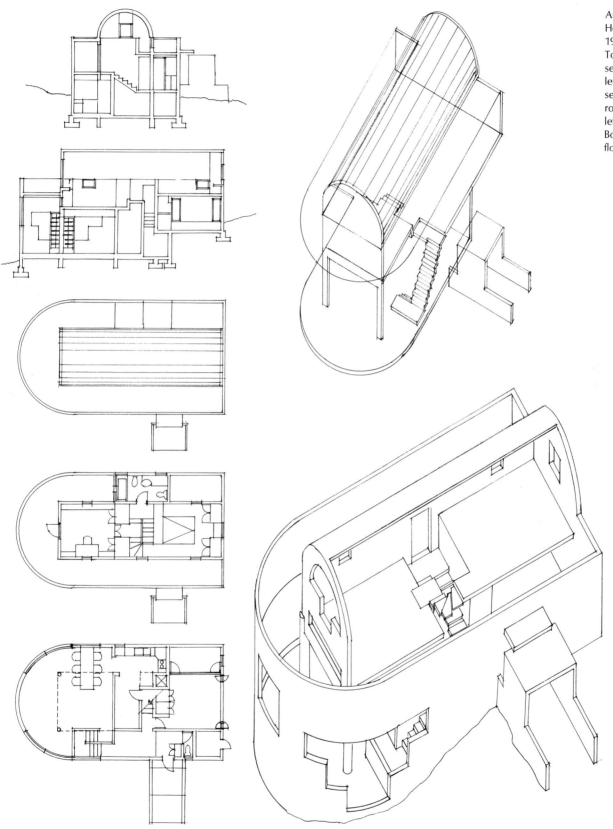

Arata Isozaki, Yano House, Tokyo, 1972–5
Top left; east-west section. Lower top left; north-south section. Centre left; roof plan. Lower left: first floor plan. Bottom left; ground floor plan

Arata Isozaki, H Residence, 1977
Axonometric
Gate and house, house and gate

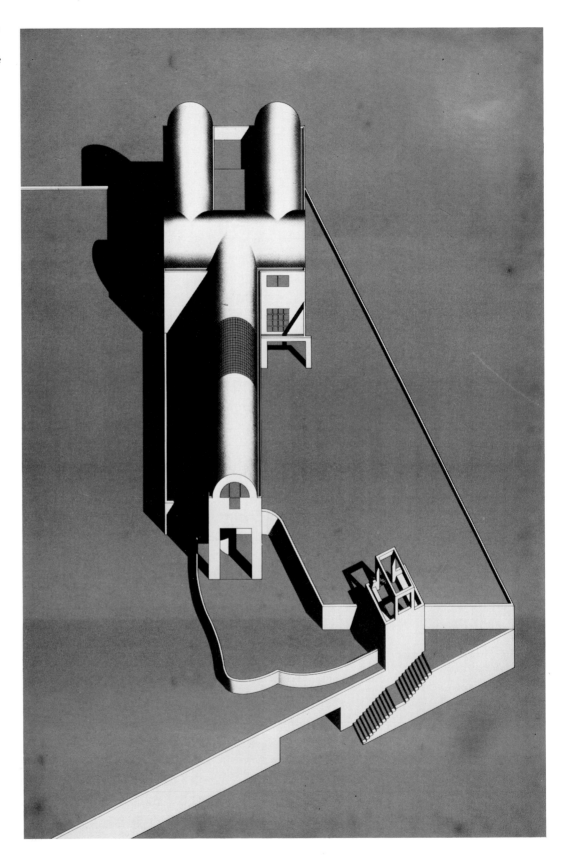

The houses of this kind of architect accost us with their polarity in plans instinct with alternate 'go' and 'stop', 'yes' and 'no', 'ritual' and 'absurd'. Before dealing with what characterises the absurd in this work, we might engage with the ritual; this kind of architect does not mince words or waste his time on sarcasm or bitter retribution, he gets on with the job of establishing a more mysterious sympathy with the city, and does so through a sustained designation of house-as-place. He capitalises on those rare moments when we see ourselves for what we are, and gives them an architectural and urban turn of phrase: this is a kind of autograph he appends to his work, not like the star signing his souvenirs but as a way of simply acknowledging his role in the affair. He dispenses with the accumulated trifles and gewgaws of architectural history – he sees them as being dreary sentiments of vanity; he bears this kind of architecture no particular malice – he smiles with a Confucian wryness, for he is out to make the world seem more interesting, not more decorated. The special consignments of phenomena we stumble across in his houses is one way he tries to implement this plan, another being the tranquil centres we find there in the depths of their liquid transparency, one could for all the world be in a Delvaux interior. *Terra incognita – terra firma*.

In the Yano house by Isozaki, the Yashiro house by Yoshida and the musician's house by Watanabe, we are reminded of the scene in Kurosawa's Derzu Uzala, set in unexplored Siberian hinterland, when the surveyor and his native guide got cut off from the rest of the expeditionary party and had quickly to build a shelter for the night as the wind rose and, the sun set . . . the odds seemed dead against the two men, their task seemed hopeless in the face of the elements of cold, wind and darkness. Dashing around, chopping down rushes and piling them up, securing them and then burrowing into the resultant nest – it all seemed implausible that those two minuscule dots of human energy could outwit the brute animism of the Steppes. Nonetheless, they secured a shelter and the couple survived the arctic night – the appearance of architecture under such circumstances testifies to its heroic and integrating role in the affairs of the elements. Dyadic houses (both ritual and absurd) operate in a similar chain of events.

These houses mount a sustained attack on finitism in all its forms, architectural, philosophical and mathematical, from Aristotle and Kant to Wittgenstein. A metaphysics of the Actual Infinite is offered as a solution to the architectural dilemma – a transfinite structure is proposed which will render finitude obsolete. This Actual Infinite, whose 'well-ordered pluriverse' is approached through a triumphal avenue of open continua, is distinct from the Vulgar Infinite comprising closed continua, barren infinitesimals and divergent series. (2)

The architecture within us and that outside us – the dyadic architect draws the distinction nicely, while managing to side-step the main pot holes of Post-Metabolism: 'fantastic self-infatuation' and 'elaborate circumspection'. He manages this by always checking the ritual armature with a gesture towards the architecture-of-the-absurd. The repertoire of the 'absurd' he calls on in his houses includes the air of agility and guile in his more mannered interiors, where shadow and substance, reflection and mirror confuse the issue, stirring it into an incomprehensible agitation, like an aviary filled with tropical birds never to return to their natural habitat. From a certain angle, an Isozaki, a

Toyokazu Watanabe, Itō House,
Kyoto, 1978
Exterior

Watanabe, a Yoshida or a Tominaga house is an inaccessible place replete with multiple cancellations and beguiling illusions. The Shinohara School bleakness apparent in these houses contributes to a barren, off-stage, off-centre, mute mood: but it is not claustrophobic – the dyadic architect is just getting his own back on the stereotyped cool facades and frightening interior perspectives of modernism. His is an a-rational 'empty and marvellous' space of paradoxes, and he employs typical emblems of absurdity in his search for something larger; he envisages his houses to be a veritable 'relativity for the layman', exhibiting an apparent equivalence between mass and energy, and each could quite easily be mistaken for an Atomic Clock.

In conclusion

One is entitled to ask that a house should be something other than a fine intellect which

Interior
The architect has written;
'This house consists of wooden
part and concrete part, and the
former, the residential part of the
second floor, is sandwiched by
the latter. The room with circular
stairs on the first floor is the
place for the client, the retired
teacher, to play and study with
children in the summer and
winter vacation. He calls this
room a little Coloseum.'
A true synthesis of negation and
celebration; cool white spaces
and warm womb-like hearth,
hard lines and soft contours,
mechanical details and rich
lighting; this house is a
composite of the houses of
Shinohara, Mozuna, Hara,
Isozaki . . .

makes us forget. There are tasks more urgent, more pressing, more deserving of our attention than the manipulation of forms in harmonic constellations. Chinese puzzles of form, and delicate mandarin subtleties seem misplaced, futilely pointing towards the architect's elevated ideas of himself. But real genius is rarer than the architect fancies, and hangs on a judgement that his age is not qualified to give. The lofty self-adulatory way certain architects go about designing ends up with pompous and tautological parodies, at best eccentrically portentous, at worst mediocrity personified.

If in the course of this book you might have lived some of the real and urgent alternatives, then the groupings, the classifications, the anthropologies, the beads of sweat might have been worthwhile.

AFTERMATH

The New Japanese House:

(to be read aloud)

The new Japanese house is a physical response to the unseen. We cannot remember without it, we could not survive – it affords a way of negotiating our way through time./ Locational attempts – the new Japanese house as a land marking system. Methods of marking the earth's surface – surface and volume notions: which preceded which? The problem of origins has to do with internal as well as external matters./ Space tends to take the shape of its container./ The new Japanese architecture – the measurement and description of pieces of land./ Matter – whatever occupies space – the new Japanese house is high density matter. Are the basic properties of matter the basic properties of this new house? Matter is also defined as whatever communicates itself to the senses in some way – surely this must be the new Japanese house too!/ Is it an expression of the equality of two entities, man and environment?/ The new Japanese architecture can be created in any form except those contrary to logic./ The freedom of the designer lies in the impossibility of knowing what the future holds./ A house agrees with reality or not: it is true or false./ My aim is to include all the more or less interesting words to do with this new architecture./ The new Japanese house; consecration of the instant; it is knowledge, power, abandonment and salvation for some. An operation capable of changing the world, the new Japanese architectural activity can be revolutionary./ The new Japanese architecture reveals this world by creating another – its own. It isolates; it divides. Invitation to the journey; return to the home. Inspiration, respiration, muscular and cerebral exercise. Hymn to the void; dialogue with absence – tedium, anguish and despair nourish it. Prayer, litany, epiphany, presence. Exorcism, conjuring, magic. Sublimation, compensation, condensation of the unconscious. Historic expression of races, states, classes. It denies history; at its core all objective conflicts are resolved and man at last acquires consciousness of being something more than transient. Experience, feeling, emotion, intuition, undirected thought. Result of chance; fruit of calculation. Brother of anthropology. Making things in a particular way – obedience to rules; creation of others. Imitation of the ancient, copy of the real, copy of a copy of the idea. Madness, ecstasy, logos. Return to childhood, coitus, nostalgia for paradise, for hell, for limbo, for the in-between. Play, work, ascetic activity. Confession. Disguising. Innate experience. Vision, music, symbol – the eye and the ear responding to each of its details in turn, from column to roof, tile to window. Teaching, morality, example – a didactic, monumental new Japanese architecture that serves as permanent warning./ Revelation, dance – the Baroque. Monologue – the International style. Voice of the people – Vernacular. Language of the chosen, word of the solitary. Pure and impure, complex and contradictory, form and no form, sacred and damned, built and yet not built, sheltering but threatening, popular and of the minority, collective and personal, naked and clothed, spoken, painted, written; it shows every face, but there are those who say it has no face; the new Japanese architecture is a mask that hides the void, a veil over the grim reality./ Freedom, spontaneous activity, transformation and chains. History overturned and restored again in an instant – a long solitary gesture that gathers together bits from far and wide in the creation of a building./ Architecture as something lived and suffered – we have no choice but to cling on tight./ When we question the building about the existence of architecture, are we not arbitrarily confusing architecture and building? There can be architecture without buildings – a cave, the covering of trees, a secluded spot at the heart of a forest./ The new Japanese house as the condensation of powers and circumstances alien to the designer's creative will./ We face something strange: a work. A product of the joint resources of mind and matter, each a stark revelation of man and the way he exploits his habitat. It is as customary and as strange as anything of man's output./ The building is architecture standing erect. A building is an organism that contains, stimulates or emits architecture. The form and the substance are the same./ How can we lay hold of the new Japanese architecture if each building reveals itself as something different and irreducible?/ Any activity is susceptible to the creation of a need for a building./ Sociology, psychology, philosophy are indispensable if we want to study the new Japanese house, but they can tell us nothing about its ultimate nature./ Is architecture the sum of all buildings? What justification is there for calling Monta Mozuna's Anti-dwelling, the Santa Sophia and the Todas' menstruation hut architecture? This diversity stems from history. Each building is a unique object, created by a technique that dies at the very moment of creation. Each building is part formula, part invention: the proportions of these are determined by history, the determination of the architect and circumstance; this is all part transmissible, part inscrutable./ The collective and private myths are compounded into an amalgam that suggests such sweeping topics as the new Japanese architecture and such minutiae as the architect himself, pencil in hand./ The house arises simultaneously out of nothing and out of the commonplace, and in the middle of this it is impossible to escape from meaning – does one aspire to the unequivocal or a system of divergent meanings? (Symmetry versus asymmetry.)/ Is the new Japanese house a victory over matter, or a setting free of matter?/ The elements of architecture, as soon as they go together in the making of a building, without ceasing to be what they are (bits and pieces of communication), turn into something else. That change does not consist in an abandonment of their original nature, but in a return to it. To be 'something else' means to be the 'same thing', the thing itself, that which is, really and originally . . . the materials of the building are not purely and simply wood, stone, brick; they are the incarnation of something that transcends and surpasses them. An ambivalence arises: the element is completely that which it is (scale form, texture) and it is also something else – image. The new Japanese architecture transforms matter into image. Without ceasing to be language (sense and its transmission) the building is something beyond language; it is the thing itself, sparkling or opaque, denying the world of utility. It is this capacity as image that permits Mozuna's Anti-dwelling, Toledo cathedral, a Tibetan monastery and a squatter's settlement to be called architecture. As images, buildings, without ceasing to be themselves, transcend architecture as a given system of historical meanings./ History is a flux, but architecture's amplitude is greater./ Each building, each house, is unique./ All architecture, with greater or lesser intensity, is latent in each work./ A magnetic object, a secret meeting place of many opposing forces – capitalism, socialism; the few, the many. The house, especially, gives us access to the architectural experience. The house is a possibility open to all men, regardless of their temperament, mentality or disposition. The house is just this; a possibility, something that is only animated by contact with the user./ The house is produced in history, is history and at the same time denies history – the user relives an image, denies succession, and overflows time./ The house mediates between synchronic and diachronic conceptions of time, and one stands before it, palpitating./ A house, through the corridors that connect it to one or more of its prototypes, provides a means of reaching pure time, an immersion in the original waters of existence./

APPENDIX ONE

The New Japanese House:

The story begins in 1858, the Meiji Restoration, when after two hundred years of isolation, Japan was once more opened up – foreign traders, emissaries, *et al* could enter once more, and their influence quickly spread; Western institutions sprang up and buildings to accommodate them were designed in direct imitation of Beaux Arts precedent. There was little architectural interest in the single house at that time; projects were mainly of the type to fuel the engines of Japan's nascent economy, but nonetheless Western furnishings slowly filtered through into what were otherwise traditional Japanese houses, wings in a Western style came to be added, and occasionally whole new houses in an imported manner erected. By stealth, the Western house took over the Japanese architect's imagination as the only alternative to the native domestic tradition.

At the turn of the century, in Kyoto, Koji Fujii was the first to begin to rethink from the natural features of the Japanese house; by an exacting scientific method he combined traditional column and partition arrangements with the rationality of Western chair-style living (Five Experimental Houses, 1920s). Chuta Ito, in Tokyo (Asano House 1909, Irisawa House 1923, Shiraishi House 1935) also insisted on deriving the best from Japanese experience, as did Keiji Goto (Minami House 1918), and Isoya Yoshida.

From 1915 to 1920, Arata Endo and Antonin Raymond, who had both worked with Frank Lloyd Wright, turned out copybook houses in a modern vein, as did the Japan Secession Group, formed in 1920 by Sutemi Horiguchi. Slightly later, the houses of Maeyakawa, Taniguchi Sakakura and Murano affected a cool off-white internationalism; the Bauhaus was a strong influence, several architects having studied there.

For the most part, these houses were restricted to affluent intellectuals and architects themselves – it wasn't until the 1950s that the modern house went downmarket. At that moment, with the withering away of the feudal order and lessening of domestic ceremony, the Japanese house came to be more thoroughly modernised, through the separation of functions, the centralisation of the wife's work space, etc. Kiyoshi Ikebe and Kiyoshi Seike were instrumental in this process. However, the planning was still articulated around point supports and lightweight screens were the order of the day – it wasn't until the economic boom of the 1960s that heavier wall systems came to be employed and the material life of the house came to be seriously appraised. This set the stage for moving on from the modest functionalism of the 1950s to the more self-conscious houses of the 1960s (Shinohara, Aida, Takeyama, Suzuki, Shin, Kikutake), to the plural metaphysics of dwelling that characterises the 'House' of the 1970s (Itō, Mozuna, Watanabe, Fujii, Hara, Ando).

APPENDIX TWO

The New Japanese House:

1858–1900	Lack of interest in house, mainly civic projects; few additions in foreign style to Japanese houses, some Western styled houses, sometimes for foreign traders
1909	Chuta Ito, Asano House
1918	Frank Lloyd Wright, Yamamura House, Ashiya Keiji Goto, Minami House
1920s	Koji Fujii, Five Experimental Houses, Kyoto Goichi Takeda, Arata Endo Houses, Tokyo
1923	Chuta Ito, Irisawa House
1930	Sutemi Horiguchi, Yoshikawa House
1931	Antonin Raymond, Troedson House
1934	Sutemi Horiguchi, Okada House
1935	Takeshi Ichiura, Abe House Iwao Yamawaki, Own House
1936	Chikatada Kurata, Konisho House Sutemi Horiguchi, Nakanishi House
1937	Isoya Yoshida, Kineya House Bunzo Yamaguchi, Kobayashi House
1939	Sutemi Horiguchi, Wakasa House
1942	Seichi Shirai, Shimaka Lodge

1950	Junzo Sakakura, Kano House
	Takasama Yoshizaka, Own House
1952	Masako Hayashi, House for Mr O
	Kiyoshi Ikebe, Two Consecutive Houses
	Kiyoshi Seike, Saito House
1953	Kiyoshi Seike, Miyagi House
1959	Kiyonori Kikutake, Sky House
1960	Junzo Sakakura, House With No Front
1961	Kazuo Shinohara, Chigasaki House
1962	Kazuo Shinohara, Umbrella House
1963	Kiyoshi Ikebe, PIX2
1964	Nikken Sekkei, Mountain Lodge
1966	Jun Suzuki, Triple Function House
	Jun Suzuki, House in Two Sections
	Junzo Sakakura, Bhrwani Residence
	Takamitsu Azuma, Own House
1967	Takafumi Aida, Artist's House
	Ren Architects, Alice in Wonderland House
	Tokuji Imai, Villa Lego
	Minoru Takeyama, A House with a Gallery
	Makoto Suzuki, Ishigame Residence
	Hayashi and Tomita, Exploding Space
	Mitsuru Senda, Black House
	Kazuo Shinohara, House for Mr Yamashiro
1968	Y. Hosaka, House for Yamaguchi
	Shinichi Okada, Own House
	Kiyoshi Seike, Tsuboi House
	Shozo Uchi, Weekend House
1969	Mayumi Miyawaki, Own House
	Kazunari Sakamoto, House Made of Boxes
	Ren Architects, Dentist's House
	Makoto Suzuki, GAH6812
	Takamitsu Azuma, Akatsuka House
1970	Eiji Musha, House with Fountain
	Kazunari Sakamoto, House at Minase
	Jun Itami, House at Shimizu
	Kazuo Shinohara, Mr Shino's House
1971	Mayumi Miyawaki, Blue Box House
	Minoru Takeyama, House for Three Families
	Kazunari Sakamoto, House at Nobuto
	Urbot, Aluminium House

Atelier R, House at Kataseyama
Kazuo Shinohara, Cubic Forest
Kazuo Shinohara, Repeating Crevice
Kazuo Shinohara, Sea Staircase

1972   Hiroshi Hara, Awazu House
Mayumi Miyawaki, Kanno Box
Itsuko Hasegawa, House at Yaizu
Takefumi Aida, Nirvana House
Takefumi Aida, Annihilation House
Hiroyuki Asai, House with Slanting Wall
Yasufumi Kijima, House at Tateshima

1973   Mayumi Miyawaki, Green Box 2
Mayumi Miyawaki, Triangular Box Mountain Lodge
Susumu Takasuga, Kiyohara House
Jun Itami, House with Wall Torn Open
Hiromi Fujii, Miyajima House
Yasufumi Kijima, White House
Yasufumi Kijima, Villa on a Hillside
Kazumasa Yamashita, Villa Attis

1974   Kazumasa Yamashita, Nagahara House
Takefumi Aida, House Like a Die
Kazuo Shinohara, House at Seijo
Kazuo Shinohara, House at Higashi Tamagawa
Kazuo Shinohara, House at Kugahara
Kazunari Sakamoto, House at Nagareyama
Minoru Takeyama, Row House
Yuzuru Tominaga, Inner Void
Koichi Sone, Lakeside Study

1975   Akira Muto, RM–NT Residence
Jun Itami, India Ink House
Jun Itami, Blank Space House
Hironori Shirasawa, House at Kitayama
Biken Architects, Heaven and Earth House
Shiro Kiramata, T Mountain Lodge
Dam Dan, Fantasy Villa

1976   Kazuhiro Ishii, 54 Windows
Hiromi Fujii, Todoroki House
Urbot, Black Recurrence
Takefumi Aida, Stepped House

1977   Kazuo Shinohara, House in Uehara
Masako Kayashi, House on a Cliff
Shin Toki, Villa K

Toyō Itō, House in Nagano
Tadao Ando, Bansho Residence

This chronology is provisional, not exhaustive.

APPENDIX THREE

An Analysis of Yuichiro Kojiro's 'Japan's Contemporary Houses'

Occupation of owner	Number	%	Traditional	Modern	Composite
company executive	22	29	6	10	6
company president	12	16	2	6	4
hotel or restaurant owner	3	4	1	2	0
district attorney	1	1·5	1		
accountant	1	1·5		1	
doctor	2	3	1	1	
university lecturer	3	4	1	1	1
critic/writer	2	3		1	1
illustrator/painter/designer	8	11		4	4
journalist	2	3	1	1	
architect/engineer	11	15	1	9	1
film director/actor	2	3	1	1	
T.V. director	1	1·5		1	
astronomer	1	1·5	1		
jeweller	1	1·5	1		
diplomat	1	1·5		1	

It's interesting that company executives and presidents share with architects a preference for the modern. This is symptomatic of the high rate of obsolescence and renewal that characterises Japanese cities. There is a constant search for newness and uniqueness, both good aids in the face of fierce competiton.

REFERENCES

Titles of publications, when given, are abbreviated, serving to refer the reader to the bibliography proper. When no page number is given, the work referred to should be consulted for the general argument rather than a specific point.

Preliminaries
1. Czaja, AAJ, p. 63
2. Smithson, pp. 276–285
3. Brown, p. 28

Ch. 1.
1. Smith
2. Fawcett, *New Nature*
3. Fawcett, *The Castle Builders*
4. Fawcett, *Ideology and Epiphany*

Ch. 2.
1. Merleau-Ponty
2. Rajadhon, p. 3
3. Frankfort, pp. 84–5
4. Proust, *Swann's Way*
5. Thomas
6. Bellah, p. 218
7. Tambiah, p. 92
8. Quarantelli and Davis
9. Needham, pp. 119–120
10. Bachelard
11. Faegre
12. Inn, p. 10
13. Hastings
14. Sadler
15. Sartre

16. Berger, p. 150
17. Abe, p. 14
18. Heidegger, *L'Art et L'espace*, p. 20
19. Zenji, p. 109
20. Rajneesh, p. 13
21. Bashō, p. 98

Ch. 3
1. Munro
2. Czaja, *Gods of Myth and Stone*, p. 60
3. Speidel, Thesis, p. 281
4. Shunsuke, p. 42
5. Aston, *Nihongi*, p. 369
6. Yanagita, p. 119
7. Yanagita, p. 97
8. Yanagita, p. 126
9. Takatori, p. 160
10. Casals, p. 44
11. Iwata and Schaafama, p. 121
12. Czaja, *Gods . . .*, p. 49
13. Kirby, p. 237
14. Yanagita, pp. 93–5
15. Mukaiyama, pp. 132, 232
16. Casals, p. 27
17. Hosen
18. Speidel, *Pilgrimages*, p. 19

19. Shunsuke
20. Sansom, p. 46
21. Takatori, p. 62
22. Shunsuke
23. Küchler, pp. 121–2
24. Takatori, pp. 57–8
25. Takatori, p. 153
26. Shunsuke
27. Takatori, p. 61
28. Speidel, Thesis, p. 302
29. Aston, *Shinto*, p. 168
30. Puini and Dickens, p. 445
31. Speidel, Thesis, p. 279
32. Aston, *Shinto*, p. 314
33. Takatori, p. 236
34. Williams, p. 16
35. U.K.E., p. 5
36. Gogol, p. 31
37. Gogol, p. 32
38. Solzhenitsyn, p. 26

Ch. 4.
 1. Hara, pp. 11–12

Ch. 6.
 1. Abe, p. 295
 2. Nitschke
 3. Bellah, p. 227
 4. Fawcett, *Hiromi Fujii*
 5. Kinoshita
 6. Ishii
 7. Vernon

Ch. 7.
 1. Fawcett, *Anarchist's Guide*
 2. Mozuna, p. 317
 3. Wilhelm
 4. Wilson, pp. 14–15
 5. Le Corbusier, p. 87

Ch. 8.
 1. Proust, *Within a Budding Grove*, p. 60
 2. Bernadete

Aftermath
The reader is referred to the work of Octavio Paz: this section is an architectural homage to his poetics.

BIBLIOGRAPHY

K. Abe, *The Ruined Map*, Tuttle, Tokyo, 1971.

W. G. Aston (tr.), *Nihongi*, Tuttle, Tokyo, 1975.

W. G. Aston, 'Shinto', *Logos*, Tokyo, 1968.

G. Bachelard, 'The House Protects the Dreamer', *Landscape*, Winter, 1963/4.

Bashō, *The Narrow Road to the Deep North*, Penguin, Harmondsworth, 1977.

R. N. Bellah, 'Liturgy and Experience', in *Roots of Ritual*, ed. J. D. Shaughnessy, W. D. Eerdmans, Michigan, 1973.

P. Berger, *Invitation to Sociology*, Doubleday, N.Y., 1963.

J. A. Bernadete, *Infinity*, Clarendon Press, Oxford, 1964.

N. O. Brown, *Life Against Death*, Sphere, London, 1968.

U. A. Casals, *The Five Sacred Festivals of Ancient Japan*, Sophia University, Tokyo, 1967.

E. M. Czaja, 'Antonin Raymond Artist and Dreamer', *Architectural Association Journal (AAJ)*, Vol. 78, No. 863, June/July 1972.

M. Czaja, *Gods of Myth and Stone*, Weatherhill, Tokyo, 1974.

A. Faegre, *American Dwellings*, unpublished Master's thesis, M.I.T., 1976 . . . quoting Thoreau.

C. Fawcett, 'Ideas That Operate Between Floor and Ceiling, The Projects of Fujii Hiromi', *Architectural Association Quarterly (AAQ)* Vol. 6, No. 2, 1974.

C. Fawcett, 'An Anarchist's Guide to Modern Architecture', *AAQ*, Vol. 7, No. 3, 1975.

C. Fawcett, 'The Castle Builders of Japan', *Architectural Design (AD)*, Vol. XLX, June, 1975.

C. Fawcett, 'Ideology and Epiphany: The Air Conditioned Temples of Japan's New Religions', *AAQ*, Vo. 10, No. 4, 1978.

C. Fawcett, 'New Nature New Luxury', *Toshi Jutaku*, No. 89, March, 1975.

H. Frankfort, *Before Philosophy*, Penguin, Harmondsworth.

N. Gogol, *Dead Souls*, Airmont, New York, 1966.

H. Hara, 'An Interview With David Stewart', *AAQ*, Vol. 10, No. 4, 1978.

Hastings, *Encyclopedia of Religion and Ethics*, Clark, Edinburgh, section on 'Home'.

M. Heidegger, *L'Art et L'espace*, Erker-Verlag, St. Gallen, 1969.

S. Hosen, *Nihon no Minzoku*, Nara Ken, (*Japanese Folklore – Nara Prefecture*), Dai Ichi Hoki Shuppan, Tokyo, 1972.

H. Inn, *Chinese Houses and Gardens*, Hastings House, New York, 1950.

K. Ishii, *Sukiya Concept*, GA Houses No. 4, ADA Edita, Tokyo, 1978.

K. Iwata and H. Schaafama, *Mo Chotto de Eigo wa Hanaseru (You Too Can Speak English)*, Kobunsha, Tokyo, 1973.

M. Kinoshita, *Sukiya*, Shokokusha, Tokyo, 1965.

R. J. Kirby, *Ancestral Worship in Japan*, Transactions of the Asiatic Society of Japan, Vol. 38, 1910–12.

L. W. Küchler, *Marriage in Japan*, Transactions of the Asian Society of Japan (Yokohama), Vol. 13, 1885.

Le Corbusier, *My Work*, Architectural Press, London, 1960.

M. Merleau-Ponty, *L'Oeil et L'Esprit*, Gallimard, Paris, 1964.

M. Mozuna, 'Ten Manifestations for the "Uchū-an" ', *GA Houses 4*, ADA Edita, Tokyo, 1978.

M. Mukaiyama, *Nihon no Minzoku, Nagano ken (Japanese Folklore – Nagano Prefecture)*, Dai Ichi Hoki Shuppan, Tokyo, 1975.

N. G. Munro, *Ainu Creed and Cult*, Columbia University, New York, 1963.

J. Needham, *Science and Civilisation in China*, Vol. IV, pt. 3, Cambridge University Press.

G. Nitschke, *Shime*, A.D., 74/12.

M. Proust, *Swann's Way*, Vintage Books, New York, 1970.

M. Proust, *Within a Budding Grove*, Chatto and Windus, London, 1976.

Puini and Dickens, *The Two Gods of Happiness*, Transactions of the Asiatic Society of Japan, Vol. 8, 1880.

Quarantelli and Davis, *Psychology Today*, February, 1972.

P. A. Rajadhon, *The Story of Thai Marriage Custom*, Thai Culture Series, No. 15, Bangkok, 1956.

B. S. Rajneesh, *No Water, No Moon*, Rajneesh Foundation, Poona, 1975.

A. L. Sadler (tr.), *The Ten Foot Square Hut (Hōjōki) and the Tales of the Heike*, Tuttle, Tokyo, 1975.

G. B. Sansom, *The Tsuredzure Gusa Yoshida no Kaneyoshi*, Transactions of the Asiatic Society of Japan, Vol. 39, 1911.

Jean Paul Sartre, *The Reprieve*, Penguin, Harmondsworth, 1968.

T. Shunsuke, *Ie no Kami (Gods of the House)*, Tankosha, Kyoto, 1972.

H. Smith, unpublished paper comparing Tokyo with London. (Princeton University, Department of History.)

P. Smithson, 'Form Above All', *AAJ*, Vol. 78, No. 870, March 1963.

A. Solzhenitsyn, *August 1914*, Penguin, Harmondsworth, 1974.

M. Speidel, *Anthropological Notes on Architecture, Japanese Places of Pilgrimage*, pt. 12, A and U, 75/12.

M. Speidel, *Semiotic Considerations on the Built Environment*, unpublished Ph.D. thesis, Waseda, Tokyo.

M. Takatori, *Minzoku no Kokoro (The Heart of Folklore)*, Asahi Shinbunsha, Tokyo, 1972.

J. Tambiah, *Buddhism and the Spirit Cults in North Thailand*, Cambridge University Press, 1970.

D. Thomas, *The Followers*.

U.K.E., London Issue 67, June 1978.

J. Vernon, *Inside The Black Room*, Penguin, Harmondsworth, 1966.

Y. Watanabe, 'Dragon Fort', *Japan Architect*, June 1969, Vol. 44, No. 6.

K. Wilhelm, 'From the Fantastic to the Fantasy', *AAQ*, Vol. 11, No. 1, 1979.

C. A. S. Williams, *Outlines of Chinese Symbolism and Art Motives*, Kelly and Walsh, 1932.

C. Wilson, *Mysterious Powers*, Aldus/Jupiter, London, 1975.

K. Yanagita, *About our Ancestors*, Japan Society for the Promotion of Science, Tokyo, 1970.

H. Zenji, *Yasen Kanna Jo* (tr. Shaw and Schiffer), Monumenta Nipponica, Tokyo, Vol. XIII, April–July 1957, Nos. 1–2.

INDEX